BIG DREAMS, SCARY GIANTS, AND ITTY-BITTY GRASSHOPPERS

Letting God Make His Dreams for You Come True

By Kristin Kay Johnson

Big Dreams, Scary Giants, and Itty-Bitty Grasshoppers:
Letting God Make His Dreams for You Come True
© 2013 Kristin Kay Johnson

Published by The Shepherd's Haven Ranch Publishing House
Concho, Arizona

ISBN: 978-1-940243-13-9
Library of Congress Control Number: 2013918052

Unless otherwise indicated, All Scripture taken from the King James Version. The KJV is public domain in the United States.

The Orthodox Jewish Bible fourth edition, OJB. Copyright 2002,2003,2008,2010, 2011 by Artists for Israel International. All rights reserved.

A PRAYER

Dear Heavenly Father,

You are the one who hears my prayers, who keeps His covenant of love with those who love you and obey your commands. Let your ear be attentive and your eyes open to hear the prayer I am praying before you, as I confess the sins I have committed against you. I have missed the mark of what you have called me to be. I have not always done the things you have asked me to do. I have failed to trust you, believe in you, and follow you. I have failed to love the people you came to save.

Please forgive me and set me back on the path you have laid before me. With stones of faith, repentance, love, trust, and courage, help me lay claim to the place you have chosen as a dwelling for your name—a place for people to come to you and seek your face. Thank you, Father for your grace, love, and mercy that endure forever and your compassion that never fails.

Your daughter,

Kristin

TABLE OF CONTENTS

PREFACE

Dear Reader,

I want to share with you a message about love, grace, forgiveness, the calling of God, big dreams, scary giants, and grasshoppers. Although this story weaves throughout various events in my life to illustrate the relationship God desires to have with all His children, it is not just about me. It is about God and how He intervenes in the lives of His children, demonstrates His love for them, establishes a relationship with them, shows them His plan for their lives, and then works through the circumstances in their lives to accomplish His purposes. He does this through the lives of all His children, everywhere, and throughout all history.

If this story were about me, it would not be a beautiful heroine meets proud, handsome hero, "hate-turns-to-love-and-then-everyone-is-happy" Harlequin romance type of story. My story would be more this kind: I was sort of looking for God—but in all the wrong places. I didn't really expect to find Him and wasn't really listening to His voice. My life was a mess. I blamed God, but then cried out to Him for help. He reached out to me, changed my heart, and then my life was transformed to a life of joy and purpose. (All true, but that story will have to wait for another day.) He has given me a message to share with you, and that is what this book is about, His message.

With countless books written and published by famous household names of the day, you might be wondering why you should invest your time reading a book written by an ordinary, unknown, non-famous person like me. I understand your thinking. I am not trying to be self-deprecating or self-denigrating when I say, believe me, I was tempted to just forget it. The thought crept into my mind: *Why bother writing a book that no one will read?* God's reply was forceful and immediate:

> *This is my book; my message. I* gave you this message, but it is not meant only for you, but for *them* also. *I* will draw the people whom I have chosen to hear this message. They *will* read this book. I will accomplish it. I will perform it.

If you are reading these words, it is because God has chosen you to hear His message and has drawn you to read them.

A while back, I was asked to describe the people who would read this book. The only answer I could give was: "I don't know. God just told me the book was for them and I am not sure who 'them' are. It is enough that He knows who they are and it's His job to draw them to the book." He told me that my job was to write down what He told me to write down. So there you go; this story is for you—yes, *you*. I am not privy to knowing how or why God chose you to share in this story. You may already have an intimate relationship with the Lord, spanning many years, or you may not know Him at all. I may not know you, the trials and tribulations you are going through, or what calling God has placed on your life, but God knows *exactly* who you are and all the rest. I pray that God will reveal Himself and His purposes for you as you read His message in this book.

August 1989

I first met the Lord one evening in August 1989. My youngest daughter was only a few weeks old at the time and I was suffering from long-standing, severe depression. Words cannot describe the euphoric experience, when God told me He loved me and forgave me for all my many mistakes. He told me He had a plan for my life, took me into my future, and showed me the dream of The Shepherd's Haven—and so my journey began. I will recount in greater detail this and many other experiences He led me through, but for the moment, fast forward to October 2006.

October 2006

I was feeling anxious about my job as a teacher, and some family conflicts which were overwhelming me at the time. It finally dawned on me that I had been worrying more than praying (and even then, only half-heartedly), and I started pouring my heart out to the Lord asking Him for help. After a sleepless night spent in prayer, the following morning He gave me a message I am now sharing with you. In the message, He told me I would one day write a book, more than one, actually, but, uncertain as to whether the message was actually from Him or only the longings of my own heart, I filed it away among other keepsakes and eventually forgot about it.

January 2011

Years later, in January 2011, while staying with my mother as she recuperated from surgery, God reminded me of His message, where I had put it, and told me to dig it out and read it again. I clearly heard Him tell me it was time to start writing the book. I had forgotten all about that part. *Say what? Me, write a book? But if people read it, they will know about me and who I am. You're joking, right?* Before I met the Lord, my natural inclination was to be low-key, anonymous, and unknown. As a youth, I enjoyed performing on horseback, or as a trick roping artist in a group among other performers. As an individual, however, I was not one to attract a lot of attention, and usually did not seek it. An introvert by nature, I was easily intimidated and painfully shy. The thought of writing a book and having people know about me terrified me. For the first of what would be *many* times, He reminded me that my "giants" were only "grasshoppers" to Him, and with His help, I could write this book.

Speaking of *time*—discussing chronological events from both God's perspective and a human perspective—can be tricky. I often get stuck thinking and discussing events in linear terms of past, present, and future, but God exists separate and outside of time. He lives in the eternal present. He is the Alpha and Omega and knows the end from the beginning. In human terms, the dream He gave me had not yet come into being, but from His perspective, The Shepherd's Haven already existed in its fullest, most complete expression. When He showed me the dream, He showed it to me as it *already existed.* Standing on the alpha side of the Lord, I have been waiting, watching, and praying for the dream to be fulfilled since August 1989. This is an inside joke between the Lord and me. He has a quirky sense of humor, I have discovered. You will agree with me as I share the rest of the story.

One example of His sense of humor is when the Lord informed me that He loves the books I have written—before I had even constructed the first sentence of this, my first book. He has already "read" *all* of my books (all as in *multiple, more than one*). (Yeah, this thought makes me nervous.)

Having established that I was going to write a book, the subject of which I had not a clue, I actually asked the Lord what it would be about. His reply was: "You aren't writing it. It has already been written. It just hasn't been published yet." Of course, being skeptical and dubious, *I* remember thinking, *I don't know, it doesn't look very "already written" to me. I am looking at an empty page, (other than what you just read), and I do not really see where this book is going to come from without a lot of work."* His response was: "That depends on which side of the Alpha and Omega you are standing on." I didn't get it at first, but then I did. (Funny! I swear I could actually hear Him chuckle. See what I mean about His quirky sense of humor?) Then He told me, "I have read your books. They are very good. I enjoy them. They will serve nicely to accomplish my purposes."

Okay. I can do this, I agreed. So I started having conversations with God and wrote down what He told me to write down. I did this pretty well for a few months, but then, as the subject matter He addressed became more personal and touched on painful areas of my life, I was no longer certain about the whole project. I stopped spending much time working on it, and spent even less time talking to the Lord about it. Of course, I made all kinds of plausible excuses to

God: "My mother is recuperating from surgery," "I have to help Mom move," "We're moving from Florida to Arizona," "I'm tired and busy... and stressed out," and the list went on. He didn't buy any of them and gently chided me that I was stalling. He knew that I wanted to do His will, but a big part of me was afraid to write this book.

I am afraid of failure but also of success. I fear getting ahead of God and trying to force things to happen outside of His will, but I also fear forgetting Him, or taking credit for success that belongs to Him. I fear following the wrong voice and going against the Lord, or worst of all, doing *nothing* He calls me to do. All of these are expressions of the underlying sins of doubt, unbelief, lack of trust, and reticence to follow *Him*.

It was only a thought—a question. Doubt. Perhaps I was wrong about being called, or He had removed the calling from my shoulders and I didn't have to worry about it anymore. Had I made it all up? Had God never told me to write this book or start The Shepherd's Haven? Maybe it was my dream and not His. Part of me was relieved at the thought.

I was conflicted. *Why would God give a dream like this to someone like me? I mean, look at me! I am a* **nobody**. *I am already over fifty years old, too old to even do this anymore. I have no ministry, no website, no mailing list, no money, no reputation, no platform—nothing. Zip. Zilch. Nada. Besides, I mess everything up!* Right then, God spoke: "**You would be surprised at what I can do through a 'nobody' like you!**"

Funny thing. Though I know God knows everything, it often fails to register with me that He literally KNOWS EVERYTHING and HEARS EVERYTHING—even the silent thoughts in my head. Thinking my tirade had been for my internal ears alone, this stopped me cold. *Whoa! Ummm, back up! You mean* **you** *were listening?*

Yes. Remember your Greek class? In the beginning was the Word, and the Word was with God and the Word was God.

God was the Word. I create with nothing more than my Word. I need nothing more. I spoke this world into existence. Everything that you see and the billions of things you haven't seen or even dreamed of came into existence at MY WORD. I speak worlds and universes into existence, yet sometimes you are afraid to trust ME.

I feed and clothe the small, unseen creatures you know nothing about. I know your every thought, have numbered every hair on your head, and save your tears when you cry, yet you have a hard time believing MY WORD or trusting that I can do BIG THINGS for you and in your life.

Yes, it is a lot of money, lots of land, lots of people—scary things to think about—and you hold back from starting because you feel so small and unworthy, insignificant, and think I would choose others for this and not you. I say, why NOT YOU? Years ago, I called you by name. Years ago, I gave you the DREAM—and you heard me. You know you heard me.

Yes, I heard Him, but I thought He had changed His mind. Apparently, I was wrong. The dream was first given to me, in part, when I was thirteen years old, and in greater detail just after I met the Lord, when He called me into ministry in August 1989. It is difficult to describe the dream He showed me. At the time, my youngest daughter was less than two months old, I was unemployed, broke, depressed, and felt my life was going nowhere, fast. Then shortly after I first met Him, God took me into my future and showed me what I would do with my life one day. In my youthful exuberance, I quickly jumped in, not unlike Moses, and set out to do His will...*my way.*

Not unpredictably, I messed everything up, and then, like Moses, I ran to the "back side of the wilderness" to lick my wounds. I was not ready to face the "giants" I had seen. They terrified me and I was not keen on tackling them again anytime soon. I had been gripped with fear that people would see I was flawed and sinful, and a perfect target for derision and ridicule. I am fond of the back side and don't relish engaging with the enemy, fending off fiery darts, swords, and scary things like that.

The dream God had shown me was a BIG DREAM. He hadn't given me a little, bite-sized, manageable dream that I could accomplish on my own. Nope. It was a huge, giant-sized dream that I could *never* accomplish in my own strength, or through my own knowledge, wisdom, capability, or resources. I would have to depend on Him every step of the way. To top it off, He had instilled in my heart such a fervent desire to see it accomplished that even when I have been tempted, I have not let go of it. I don't know *how* God will accomplish this dream, or *when* He will; only that He promised He would.

Do I have doubts that anyone will read this? Yes. An equally scary thought is, *Am I prepared for how my life could change if they do?* These are the giants I have been afraid to face. These are some of the reasons I have run away from both God and the giants in the past. However, when I run away from what God calls me *to be* and *to do* He gently chides me:

> Turn around. You are going the wrong way and it leads to ruin. I have not given you a spirit of fear. I am your hedge of protection. I am your shelter, your refuge. Do not be like Jonah. Do NOT run away from this. Do not be like Jeremiah or Moses and give me excuses. I will provide everything you lack, as you need it. I will be the pillar of cloud by day, and the pillar of fire by night. Giants you face are not even grasshoppers to me. I laugh at them. I still sit on my throne and laugh.

So you see, I can't run away from *Him*. I just can't. I want what God wants.

The reassuring reply came quickly: *"Just remember they are not even grasshoppers to me. I will go before you, come behind you, and*

encompass you all around." I am counting on that, Lord. Yes, defi-
nitely. I cannot do this without you.

I share my fears and feelings of inadequacy not only because I have been plagued with them throughout my life, but primarily to demonstrate the truth that with God's help, anyone can accomplish great things, despite their fears, insecurities, faults, mistakes, or ineptitude. You might also suffer from feelings of doubt, fear, guilt, worthlessness, and the like. I pray that you may be encouraged by the lessons God has taught me and the experiences He has brought me through. I am not writing this book to hold myself up as an expert in anything except having faith in God.

One day, I made the mistake of complaining to God that I didn't feel comfortable writing a book about Him, because I didn't go to seminary and get a degree in theology. His reply was something to this effect: "I AM Theos (God) and the Logos (the Word). If there is something you want to know, ask me. Now—get busy!" If you take nothing else away from this book, it is my most sincere hope that you will be confronted with the love of God, and gain the certitude that you have nothing to lose and everything to gain by believing, trusting, and following Him.

I don't have all the answers for the questions you will have as you read this book. I am simply following God and the instructions He gives me. The only thing I know for certain is that He knows what He is doing. Oswald Chambers wrote about this dilemma in his book, *My Utmost for His Highest*, in the daily devotion for January 2nd. Essentially, Chambers urges readers to go all-out for God, trust in Him entirely, and remain in perpetual wonder at what He is going to do next. God will never tell you what He is going to do next; He will only tell you who He is—a miracle-working God. This is what makes walking with God A GREAT ADVENTURE. (I encourage you to read the actual devotion—even the entire book. You will be glad you did.)

Speaking of *books.* I have one request to make of you before you read this book. Get out your favorite Bible and keep it handy, because you will need it. There are specific books and chapters in the Bible that I would like for you to read from your own Bible. I will include passages here from the King James Version or the Orthodox Jewish Bible. By reading them in your own Bible, you will benefit from reading the accompanying text, notes, and commentary included in most Bibles, which I am not able to share here. Do not be surprised if this leads you to read other passages in the Bible as well. For example, God told me to read Deuteronomy 28, which led to me reading the whole book of Deuteronomy. Because Deuteronomy 28 is such a long chapter, I tried to share it in a limited fashion, but couldn't decide which parts to share and which parts to leave out. (Sheesh! How does one limit God's Word?) Then He told me this was not a time for cut and paste, so for every book or chapter I reference, I include here in its entirety.

One last technical note, (well, two actually). Throughout this book, I often refer to the first names of people only, or otherwise obscure their personal information in order to protect their identity and privacy. I use real names of only those who have given me express permission to do so. Also, I have not included any pictures in this book, because they would be in black and white, and I want you to see them in color. I am putting all of the pictures and videos on my FaceBook, YouTube and Twitter pages for you to enjoy in full color. I hope you will look for them and enjoy them. The addresses are given at the end of the book.

This book is *somewhat* a chronological narrative, told through an eclectic mixture of emails, devotions, commentaries, and various other writings; all of which tell of how the Lord has been and is working in my life to bring The Shepherd's Haven to reality. Several of the writings were composed years ago, in different styles, intended for various audiences. Some were school assignments, written in an academic style, but most were not so formal. Taken individually, you may wonder why I included some of them in this compilation, but taken as a whole, my hope is that you will understand why God insisted I include them. (Please recall the point I made earlier regarding the difference between our human, linear perception of time and God's perception. He moves throughout time whenever and wherever He wants, but He lives and speaks in the *present*. In our linear time perception, the dream hasn't been accomplished *yet*, but this is where YOU come in (you who know who you are). The Lord will fill in the details for you as you read.

God has not shown me the whole picture of what The Shepherd's Haven is meant to be. He has given me only a glimpse of parts of it—enough for me to know I cannot accomplish any of it on my own. Only God, who alone knows the end from the beginning and controls the fulfillment of the dream, can make it a reality. Many other people will be involved, but only God knows who He intends to draw in to share in this undertaking. I am merely following His instructions and the rest is up to Him. God is either the author of this message or He is not. He is either behind this or He is not.

If He is, then even a *nobody* like me can write an international bestseller, and a *somebody* like you can hear His voice calling you to step out in faith to join us and help make The Shepherd's Haven a reality. God, Himself, is building a multi-location "place" to draw all people unto Him. (Please listen to your heart to hear His view of all of this.) As you read this book, I believe you will see God's fingerprints and sense the power of the story He is using to draw people like you to help build The Shepherd's Haven.

Kristin Kay Johnson

Chapter One

FROM THE BEGINNING:
MY EARLY YEARS

Many of the events in my childhood, teen, and early adult years were traumatic and painful. I made more than my share of mistakes. Still, God has used my life experiences and mistakes to shape me into the person He wants me to become and teach me about His grace. The particular mistakes you and I have made are, in His eyes, irrelevant. The relevant question is, "Are you reconciled with Him?" His grace goes far deeper than any and every mistake you've ever made.

Here are some basic facts about me: I was born Kristin Kay Hoffman in Denver, Colorado, at Presbyterian Hospital on December 27, 1961. My parents are Edward Dean (now deceased) and Claudia Arlyne Hoffman. I have two younger brothers, Blake Harold and Lance Edward, and an older sister, Esther Julyne, who suffers from mental retardation.

When I turned nine, I began training and performing with an equestrian youth performing group, Westernaires. I spent all day every Saturday, all year long, and many additional evenings during summer breaks, in the classroom learning everything about horses, (i.e. breeds, colors, first aid, proper nutrition and grooming), and individual team drills. I also spent countless hours in the arena, practicing drills with my teammates. Throughout the year, though especially during the summer, we frequently performed in parades and shows throughout the state of Colorado.

SHOWTIME. There is nothing like it. Dazzling lights and fluorescent, flashy costumes. Loud, exuberant music dances in your soul. Electricity tingles in the air, as the capacity audience awaits your entrance. Butterflies somersault in your stomach as you enter the arena and your team performs its drill with precision and daring. The thunderous applause, almost as loud as your own heartbeat, rings in your ears, playing counterpoint to the cadence of the horses' hoof beats as you exit the arena. Those few moments in the arena are glorious.

I was thrilled to be a Westernaire for four years. I had my own horse, Blaze, and remember this as a happy time in my life. I LOVED BEING A WESTERNAIRE.

Then my world came crashing down. My father died when I was thirteen, just three weeks before Christmas and my fourteenth birthday—an apparent suicide. I was devastated. I still tried to function "normally" in the world, for all appearances, though internally, my heart was shattered—numb. I cannot put words to the pain that gripped me.

A year later, leaving my sister in a group home in Lakewood, Colorado, we moved to Tulsa, Oklahoma, where my mother married a man with a son and daughter. Three weeks later we lost most of our possessions in a house fire.

Disappointment struck like lightning. There was no Westernaires. Nothing. No drill team for kids that I could find. Yes, there were a few saddle clubs, but most of them were for adults, not kids. Few of them, if any, were drill teams. There were a few horse shows where horses were judged on confirmation, breeding, and training, and riders were judged on riding ability, but this required an extremely expensive horse—my second-grade mare just wouldn't do.

There were other problems—huge problems. Though I liked my new step brother and step sister well enough, my mother's new husband drank alcohol—a lot of it. They fought all the time—violently. Life was miserable for all of us children. Our parents would share a love-hate relationship that spanned roughly thirty years—divorcing and reconciling twice before finally parting company.

I attended Jenks High School in Jenks, Oklahoma. I made a few close friends there who were emotionally supportive. They helped me to hang on. I still stay in touch with some of them. I hope they realize how much their friendship meant and still means to me.

I was also privileged to have some amazing teachers. They will never know how much they meant to me, and how much I looked up to them. I loved them—even my cranky Algebra teacher who never understood why I just couldn't get the whole math thing. I will never forget her. She is the one I think about when I savor the irony that I became a math teacher—me, perhaps her worst student.

I felt rebellious, hurt, and angry. At times, I did things that were stupid and wrong, and hurt myself. I didn't want to be rebellious. I wanted to be a good student and an obedient, helpful daughter. My mom needed me and I wanted to be there for her, but I also wanted to escape from all the pain. So I escaped into my studies.

I enrolled in every business and college preparatory course I was able to take. I also loved creative writing and enjoyed taking writing classes. I was on the newspaper/yearbook staff and served as an editor for the yearbook. In my junior year, I was one of nine students in Oklahoma to receive the National Council of Teachers of English Award. Aside from that, however, I was a mediocre student, especially in math and science. (Okay, abysmal, would be more accurate.)

However, because I was one of nine finalists to receive the National Council of Teachers of English Award, I was offered college scholarships from a number of prestigious colleges. I chose to attend St. John's College, a small, private liberal arts college in Santa Fe, New

Mexico. The required curriculum at St. John's centered on the classics, with a heavy focus on math, science, and philosophy.

I am not sure how I managed to survive all four years, but am so thankful I was able to attend such an amazing college. I loved being a student at St. John's. In my junior year there, I received a community scholarship and served for three years as the president of the St. John's Film Society. I was shy and quiet, but active in class activities. Plus, while there, I managed to learn Algebra—*finally!*

Chapter Two

A CLOSE ENCOUNTER WITH GOD

After graduating from St. John's College, I planned to join the Peace Corps and head off for destinations and adventures unknown. Instead, I got married on August 18, 1984. Katrina Marie was born on September 1, 1987, and Heather Anne was born on June 18, 1989. I had just lost a *great* job with Daylight Corporation (a donut supplies manufacturing company), because I had been seriously ill with asthma for a year, even ending up in the hospital with pneumonia for four days before Heather was born. I was terminated due to medical reasons. (Thanks guys, I really needed that.) This led to *major* depression, joined with the post-partum blues.

August 1989

There I was with two young babies to take care of, major depression to deal with, and my life was generally yucky. It led me to question *Why am I even here, anyway?* I felt like a square peg trying to fit into a round hole—unable to cope with my responsibilities as a wife and mother. I was drifting along, not knowing what I should do with my life, with no convictions to guide me.

In spite of four years of college, and having asked questions and sought answers about God, man, and the universe, I had not connected with many answers or come to many conclusions. Emotionally, I didn't have a clue. My life was a mess and I knew it. Then one night, in early August 1989, something happened to me that I still cannot quite explain. One minute, I was in the midst of agony and depression, and the next I felt the presence of Jesus. I had heard about Him, rejected and mocked Him. But I never knew Him. But then He was there in my room with me. I felt Him. For the first time in my life, I could see the falsehood and lies that I had bought into, and I felt overwhelmed with guilt and remorse. In that moment, I understood that He really is the truth, the way, and the life. He is the Lord. I began to understand. There were no more questions, and no more excuses. Not even rational thoughts. Without any reservations, I gave my life to Him that night with great joy and thanksgiving. I felt His love and forgiveness and I felt such love and gratitude for Him that I wanted to serve Him. I just didn't know how. I was about to find out.

Chapter Three

THE BIRTH OF A DREAM

Over the next couple weeks, I stumbled along trying to pray and seek the Lord, and get to know Him. One night, soon after meeting the Lord, I had a vivid dream wherein the Lord took me into my future and showed me The Shepherd's Haven, and The Equestrianaires, a youth equestrian performing group, (the starting of which had been a dream of mine but had been dormant for over fourteen years).

Reflecting on my association with the Westernaires, I realized that it had provided me with some of the most exciting, enriching and rewarding experiences in my life. I wanted to see other young people, living outside the reach of the Westernaires, have the same opportunity to learn about and gain an appreciation for horses, as well to experience the thrill of performing for an audience—the rewards for dedication, diligence, responsibility and team effort. At first, I did not have the confidence to think that I could carry it out, but the more I prayed and thought about it, the more convinced I became that it was what I was supposed to do. It was my calling. It became an obsession.

Though I understood full well that it would be difficult and expensive to start, and would require a lot of time and energy from many people, I couldn't seem to forget the idea. I could not rationalize it out of my mind or my heart. So I committed myself to see it through—to take it as far as I could. I set off on the adventure of my life, and never looked back.

I relate here in considerable detail the events that occurred in the first few years of work on The Shepherd's Haven because I think they are important. In the beginning I was only focused on starting The Equestrianaires, and I did not have a clear vision for anything beyond that. Once I started telling people about my idea of starting The Equestrianaires, I definitely experienced a snowball effect, seeing small actions I initiated precipitate reactions which became greater with each successive action of mine. The bigger my action or steps I took, the greater the reaction. Also, I definitely had the feeling that God was helping me. I experienced so many "strange coincidences" and fortuitous, miraculous events, that I grew certain I could not accomplish as much as I did without His help.

After three years of talking to anyone who would listen to me about my dream, a handful of people, a core group, formed who believed in me and what I was trying to do. They decided that it was time to quit talking and start doing something. I needed to hold a horse camp. When a friend of mine, a deejay at one of the Christian radio stations, KCFO, found out I was going to have a horse camp, he asked to interview me on one of his broadcasts. I said "Okay, great!" I did the interview. After I got home from it, several interested people called me.

I finally held my first weeklong horse camp in August 1992. Four young people attended. They enjoyed the camp tremendously and their parents were extremely pleased. In fact, they became my initial ardent supporters. Things really started to take off. An editor of *The Tulsa Christian Times* came out, watched what we were doing, and was so impressed that she wrote an article that appeared in the September 1992 issue. After the article came out, I started receiving frequent calls from people who had read the article and were interested in what I was doing. I was beginning to build a network.

Unfortunately for me, at about the same time my ministry began taking off, my personal life was falling apart. I was experiencing extreme difficulties in my marriage and came close to divorce, so I was distracted from the ministry and did not devote any attention to it for the next three months.

On December 16, 1992, I was on my way to meet a new friend when, out of the blue, I felt like the Lord was telling me it was time to bring the Westernaires to Tulsa to put on a horse show. I wrestled with the idea, wondering whether it was my own fantasy, or if it was truly the Lord speaking to me. However, He kept me awake the entire night, instructing me on what to do and who to call, so I was fairly certain it was from Him.

The next morning, I prayed to God about bringing the Westernaires to Tulsa, asking Him to either close all the doors if it was not His will, or to open the doors and clearly show me it was His will. After praying, I called Drysdales Western Wear Store at random, and asked for Jim, their coordinator of special events. I asked him if Drysdales would be interested in sponsoring a Westernaires performance. He indicated that they would be interested and to please call him after the first of the year to discuss it further. This was my first "green light."

I then asked the Lord, "If we are supposed to have this show, where are we supposed to have it?" I felt led to call the Expo and get information on renting the Expo Pavilion, inquiring about its availability for July 24-25. The pavilion was available.

I called several friends and shared with them what I felt the Lord was calling me to do. Every single person was extremely excited and encouraging. I expected at least one person to give me a reality check and tell me I was biting off more than I could chew (which I was, and knew it), but no one did. John Marshall, my deejay friend from KCFO, got *really* excited. He just knew that this was going to be an awesome show. By noon, I was thoroughly convinced the Lord had given me all the green lights I needed to show me I was supposed to pursue the show. I was ecstatic.

I called the Westernaires and spoke to Liz, the wife of the director, and told her I would like to have them come to Tulsa, and asked
if they would consider doing so the weekend of July 24-25. She was
very excited and said she felt it would work out and that they would
be able to come. She told me to call the show chairman, Alice, and
that she would be able to set things in motion if they were able to
come. So I called Alice and invited the Westernaires to come to Tulsa
the weekend of July 24-25. As it happens, it was the *only* weekend
they had open on either side for weeks. Alice became very interested
and excited. She said she would discuss the invitation with their board
of directors at their next meeting and would get back to me after the
first of the year to let me know if they would be able to come.

A couple days later, I called an accountant I had met by accident
over two years earlier at the Mexican Fiesta in downtown Tulsa. He
specialized in nonprofit accounting, so I asked him if he would do
the incorporation and serve on my board. He told me he would be
delighted. I told him I felt it was getting close to the time to incorpo-
rate it—probably in the next week or two. At that point, I did not have
even two dimes to rub together.

On December 31, I called one family whose two children had participated in my horse camp, and asked if they would be interested
in helping me financially in getting The Shepherd's Haven and The
Equestrianaires incorporated. They said they would consider it and
get back to me.

On January 2, 1993, I received a call from Alice. She had discussed
the invitation with the board. Though they had never performed in
Oklahoma, they decided to accept the invitation. According to her,
the news spread like wildfire throughout the entire Westernaires
organization, and within an hour, *EVERYONE* was extremely excited.
I was excited, too.

Two days later, the family called me back and said they would
like to help. They asked if I would like to come pick up the check the

next night. The check was for $500, enough to get the incorporation process started.

In the process of checking out price information for advertising on TV and radio, I called KNYD radio, another Christian radio station. After explaining the reason we needed to advertise, the ad rep suggested I talk to Kim because she would probably be interested in doing a *Road Show* about The Equestrianaires and the show coming in July. They connected me to her. After telling her what was going on, she quickly said she would like to have me on the *Road Show* and, "How about January 25?" I said, "Sure!" (I later found out that this was not an easy task to get asked to be on the *Road Show*. Some ministries have tried for years—and are still trying.)

The next day, January 8, I told my contact at the Expo, Paula, about the *Road Show* interview being scheduled. She told me I had to have the $400 deposit paid and the contract approved before I could mention the show being held at the Expo Pavilion. She also said the contract approval process normally takes eight to ten days to go through all the channels.

On January 12, I held a meeting at the church, but only two other people showed up, so we scrapped the formalities and spent the time praying. We prayed specifically for God's will to be done, for the finances to meet all the needs coming up, particularly the $400 deposit if He wanted me to be on the *Road Show* to talk about the show coming to the Expo Pavilion in July. On January 17, I received my second donation of $1,500. Combined with my first donation, it was enough to pay for the entire incorporation process, including the IRS 501(c)(3) nonprofit status procedure, the $400 deposit on the Expo Pavilion, stationery printing, and other incidental expenses.

On January 19, I rented a post office box in the name of The Shepherd's Haven. On the 20th, I opened up a bank account in the name of The Shepherd's Haven, and at 4:30 p.m., I dropped off the facilities application and $400 deposit at the Expo. At 9:10 a.m. the next morning, I received a call from the Expo—the contract had been approved! I would now be able to talk about the show being held at the Expo Pavilion.

On January 25, I was interviewed on the *Road Show* for an entire hour. As I was walking in my front door after the interview, I could already hear my phone ringing off the wall. After the interview, it became increasingly difficult to get any work done because of all the people calling me. They had either heard the interview or been told about it. I had so many people call that I held a meeting on January 30 for families who were interested in participating. Roughly twenty-five families showed up, so seating was at a premium in the small church. I showed them a video of Westernaires' Horsecapades and shared with them what I hoped to accomplish in Tulsa. I began to hold weekly meetings, usually at the church, but sometimes at my house. Several families were very committed and regularly attended the meetings. I now had an organization.

Something truly wonderful began to happen. The Shepherd's Haven and The Equestrianaires took on lives of their own. The families that came to my meetings were excited and enthusiastic. They were committed to the dream and vision of The Shepherd's Haven and The Equestrianaires. They began to actively help in the planning and implementation of the show. The new, unofficial members were from all walks of life, all ages, sizes, and colors.

Over the next few months, the group met weekly to plan, organize, and work on the show. I had help from all quarters; all done on a volunteer basis. I wrote hundreds of letters, soliciting resources, financial and other. On several occasions, I was successful. On Easter weekend, I received approval for the Westernaires to stay at Cascia Hall during their stay—at no charge!

We began to receive a fair amount of publicity. I was interviewed on the *Road Show* several more times, as well as on KCFO, KXOJ, and KFOX radio. I was also interviewed several times by Jim Hill of KVOO radio. Some of these stations had signals that reached beyond

Oklahoma to several neighboring states. Later, on July 6, an article about the show appeared in *The Tulsa World*. This was in addition to several other articles which appeared in newspapers throughout the entire state.

The most amazing thing about the whole project was the way everything flowed together so smoothly during the six months that the group was together. I started out being the nominal leader in charge, and in fact, kept the position throughout the project, but it was not really a hierarchical operation. Everyone had a particular expertise and they exercised it. It wasn't a matter of asking permission, they simply suggested something to the group that might be a good idea, and if they knew how to do it and were willing to do it, they would do it if the group agreed.

The entire time the Westernaires were in town, I accompanied them. I never had to worry about things being done, or at least I *didn't* worry. Somehow, group members showed up and worked all night long, baking breads and other goodies, and prepared breakfast each morning. They were there to feed the Westernaires lunch and dinner. All of the "hidden" jobs were taken care of—not because I dictated to anyone that they needed to be done; they did them simply because they needed to be done. We did our best to treat the Westernaires like royalty. Everyone thoroughly enjoyed themselves, and worked hard. The weekend was flawless. It was magic.

There was only one flaw. The show did not earn enough money at the box office to pay all the expenses. I spent most of the next year working to pay for them out of my own pocket. Thankfully, some of the debts were forgiven, including those owed to the Westernaires. The Westernaires agreed to shoulder the expenses of coming to Tulsa and performing, requiring no remuneration or donation from me. I will always be grateful to them for this. I also plan to repay them some day for their sacrifice. I know that I could have tried to solicit more help from others to help pay the debts, and perhaps some people would have helped me do this, but I didn't because I felt too stupid and guilty to ask, after having attempted to do something so obviously stupid and irresponsible. I was so depressed and devastated that I didn't think I wanted to talk to anyone ever again, and if I asked someone for money, that would mean I had to talk to them. I wasn't able to do that for awhile. So I didn't.

It took me a long time to accept the financial failure of the show and reconcile it with how wonderful it had been in every other way. It was also difficult to look at my own immaturity and shortcomings. I went through all of the what if's (what if I had been a smart, intelligent business executive—this would have been a success), and if only's (if only I could do it over again, I would do it this way).

I finally came to a place where I realized that I am who I am, and the show was what it was—period. I had done something I felt was right at the time and given it my best effort. I had waited for twenty years for someone else to do it, but no one else had. If I had not done it, it would likely still not be done—not by some high-powered, successful business executive or anyone else. So I finally forgave myself for making a mess of everything, and realized that my mistakes didn't let me off the hook. If you are called to do something, you are called—period. Joseph made mistakes. Moses made mistakes. King David made a lot of mistakes. And what about Jonah? The lesson is we are human beings—frail and fallible. In spite of our mistakes, we still need to try to do what is right and what we feel we are called to do. If you try to run away and give up doing what you want to do the most, what is there left for you to do?

So Was it a Success?

The show may have been a very stupid idea, especially since I didn't know what I was doing, but somehow it happened anyway. In July 1993, after seven months of planning and a lot of hard work on the part of many people, we brought seventy members of Westernaires (and forty of their horses) to Tulsa to perform the Horsecapades. The show could easily have cost over $40,000, but in the end, it wound up costing only approximately $18,500 to produce (mostly because of all the free labor).

The fact that the show happened at all was a miracle. A small group of people, previously unknown to one another, came together. With no prior experience in planning such a major entertainment event, in the space of six months, they did something extraordinary, involving the logistics of bringing in seventy people and forty horses from over seven hundred miles away, providing for their needs and expenses for four days. I definitely believe that God helped us to make it happen.

As it turned out, over a thousand people attended the two shows. Hundreds of parents and children came up to me afterwards, telling me they wanted to be a part of it. But since the show was not a financial success, and I was deeply in debt, I realized I did not have the resources, motivation, or ability to continue at that time. (Once again, I found myself in a state of shock and deep depression.) The interest was definitely there, but the foundation for the organization was extremely shaky (mostly because of my lack of business management knowledge and experience).

The experience also showed me that I was getting into dangerous territory. If I continued to pursue the dream in the haphazard, ignorant way I had been, everything could get too big, too fast, while I was still trying to "wing it." If I didn't know what I was doing, I could get myself into *big* trouble. So, rather than continue and grow (albeit on shaky ground, financial and otherwise), I pulled back and tried to figure out how I could learn everything I needed to know before I started, once again, to grow the organization.

Chapter Four

SOME REFLECTIONS ON BEING A CHRISTIAN

I worked for the next couple of years as a secretary in a few differ-ent jobs, not only to help provide for my family, but also to pay off as many remaining debts from the show as I was able. For several months during that time, I also attended a class every Thursday eve-ning at The School of the Holy Spirit in Tulsa, Oklahoma.

Early one morning in March 2011 (not long after I started writing this book), during my prayer time with the Lord, He told me to go through my old papers I had written while a student at The School of the Holy Spirit. He told me to look for one paper I had written on May 4, 1995. He told me that when I wrote it, He had enjoyed it so much that He wanted to make sure I featured it prominently in my "compilation."

Funny. It had never occurred to me that God was in my audience of readers. This may be true for you as well. One side of our brain "knows" He is always with us, but it doesn't connect with the other side of our brain that He really *is* with us (duh!). He really is...and He knows what we think and write.

I tried to write this particular paper in a more scholarly mode, so keep this in mind when you read it. (I don't know if that is a warning or a plea for forgiveness ahead of time, but I will remind you that He said He loved it. Enough said.) In way of background, the assignment was to respond to the following questions: How does the "Church of Acts" (the early Church) compare with the Body of Christ today? What kinds of challenges or change of mind has this class brought in your own present life and attitudes? I responded with this:

> Mulling over these questions over the past week, I realized very quickly that entire books could be written on the first question alone. Where should I start? What should I compare? Should I compare the historical backgrounds of each and discuss how political and social factors (among others), effected certain characteristics in the Church?
>
> Do the Church of Acts or Body of Christ today include every person who claims to be a believer, or must we establish criteria that define true believers from false believers (those who just "play church")? What are the boundaries of the Church of Acts? Was that era just a phase? If so, when did it end?
>
> For instance, how do the ten churches Jesus spoke of in Revelation relate to the Church of Acts? How do those same ten churches (as archetypes) relate to the Body of Christ today? Was the Church of Acts "the remnant" the Lord has continually preserved throughout biblical history? Can we recognize that remnant in the Body of Christ today?
>
> Though I recognized early on that this subject was vast and complex, I discovered that I could not see nor focus on the essential components to this question until after I waded out into the deep and actually considered some of the many questions that floated through my mind. Were the people back then somehow different from us before they met the Lord? If so, did that make the character of their commitment after meeting the Lord somehow different from ours? Did the fact that they came from a Jewish background, what with their multitudinous rules and regulations, hold out more of

a gospel of freedom and lighter burden than ours? How has our commitment been affected by coming to the gospel after already having benefited from this freedom and lightened burden for almost 2,000 years, without even having to be a Christian (because we live in a "Christian" nation)?

Was their commitment stronger because they knew they would have to give up *everything* else in their lives in order to become a Christian? What do we have to give up? Or at least, what *do* we give up? Do we experience hardships, torment, or persecution for our faith, even to the extreme of dying for it?

I spent some time reading through *Foxe's Book of Martyrs*, hoping that acquainting myself with some early church history beyond the New Testament might shed light on this question. "Persecution" describes the early Church. Stephen and eleven of the apostles, as well as Paul, were only the first of thousands of believers to be cruelly tormented and murdered in every sadistic fashion imaginable (and many beyond our imagination). They tried to kill the Apostle John, too, by casting him into a cauldron of boiling oil, but I guess that because he hadn't written Revelation yet, the Lord needed him to stay on earth—at least until he could finish his work.

The interesting thing to note is that while Satan was striving hard to destroy the Church by continually slaughtering the saints, the Church of Acts was experiencing phenomenal growth that would put the modern Church to shame. Actually, in many parts of the world, such as China, the Church still faces tremendous opposition and persecution, yet it continues to grow. The Church appears to thrive and flourish even more when it is persecuted!

Here in the United States a different picture presents itself. Indeed, there is just as much sin and evil to contend with here, maybe more. There are plenty of people for Satan to use to accomplish his purposes. The modern Church, however, appears to be staggeringly fat and sassy. No one has actually been martyred for their faith (that I know of), though a few believers have been arrested for their unpopular insistence on condemning prevalent sinful practices of today, such as abortion, homosexuality, and others.

The popular complaint is that the Church is politically incorrect. The Church is experiencing modest, if not phenomenal growth, although entire denominations are withering on the vine. The "in" thing is to be a Charismatic, with all the prosperity and goodies that go along with that. For many of the Lord's shepherd's, the commitment of the Church of Acts has translated itself into competition. Not for new converts, mind you, (especially if they are poor, helpless, needy, or unkempt) just for dollars. The people that come with the money are of secondary importance to it. (It's easier to recycle existing believers than to go out and convert new ones.)

In the same way, commitment has lost its meaning to the flock. Rather than coming into the fold and staying put, they skirt the perimeter and continue to wander off now and again, seeking new pastures. (The grass is always greener on the other side.) The born again experience is foreign terminology in many of our churches. If anyone *claims* to heal people through the power of the Holy Spirit, he or she ends up on *PrimeTime Live* and becomes a target for the criticism of other Christians who attack them more aggressively than unbelievers do!

Charlatans capitalize on people's genuine hunger and thirst for God. They are, in fact, pretenders. But that is not my concern here, or focus. My concern is on the lukewarm, unbelieving modern Church—the one that no longer seems to believe the Holy Spirit can and does still heal people, and that the Holy Spirit is with us HERE and NOW. On the whole, it appears that Church today has lost its vital connection to Jesus—it has lost its first love.

Many churches and ministries today spend all their time collecting money to build more buildings, bigger buildings, better buildings, but neglect to build the one type of building the Lord wants them to build—holy temples inside human hearts. He desires human temples that are holy, set apart and sanctified for Him to dwell in—people who love Him and choose to serve and obey Him. More, bigger, and better buildings are fine, but not at the expense of neglecting what God really requires. God doesn't need a bigger building; just a holy one. This is an individual responsibility incumbent upon each of us—making our hearts a suitable, holy dwelling place for the Lord. This is an ongoing task that must never end because the Lord seeks many temples to dwell in. Surely this is a task worthy of our attention.

After spending years trying to pin down all the questions, opinions, sidetracks, and answers that have floated through my mind, I can conclude with certainty that the answers to every question I have ever asked ultimately remain the same: the Holy Spirit. The quality, depth of character (integrity, honesty, charity, etc.), and commitment of individuals, congregations—even the Church as a whole—is always in direct relation to the amount or depth to which they love, trust in, and rely on the Heavenly Father, Jesus, His Son and the Holy Spirit (the triune God).

I can say that over the years, I have learned many things. Most importantly, I have begun to develop a deeper, more intimate relationship with God the Father, Jesus, and The Holy Spirit. I love God more than ever before. I am more committed to serving Him than I ever have been, and I am learning to serve and obey Him joyfully. I hope that I will get to the point where I backslide and sin less and less (one can hope!).

Chapter Five

A NEW BEGINNING

In May 1995, while working as a pizza delivery driver, I fell down an entire flight of stairs, badly injuring my back. Coupling the injury and the fact I was unable to work, with a lot of additional stressors in my marriage, my husband and I separated and I decided to take my daughters to visit my family in New Mexico for awhile. After a few failed attempts at reconciliation, my daughters and I stayed in New Mexico and our marriage ended in October 1995. My daughters and I lived with my mother for the next few months until I could figure out what I needed and wanted to do with my life.

Around January 1996, I felt the need to go back to school. I looked up colleges and various programs, trying to decide what I should pursue. I had not given up the dream of The Shepherd's Haven, but I did not know how to go forward with it, either. I worked at less than subsistence-level employment, and was barely able to keep food on the table and a roof over our heads. Things were getting desperate. I knew I had not been the best student, so getting into graduate school was iffy, at best.

On April 17, 1996, I wrote the following letter:

Thomas M. P., Ph.D,
Director, Graduate Programs
Drake University
College of Business and Public Administration
208 Aliber Hall
Des Moines, IA 50311-4505

Dear Dr. P.,

I enjoyed speaking with you last week. Thank you for your words of encouragement; they meant a lot to me. As requested, you should receive letters of reference from Mr. H., and Mrs. Nancy Buchenauer within a week or two. I had a couple of classes with each of these tutors over the course of four years, and Mr. H. was my senior paper advisor.

Dr. P., I appreciate your giving me the chance to share my goals for the future and talk about my grades as a student at St. John's, and not summarily rejecting my application for admission. I do have dreams and goals for my life that I am determined to fulfill, but I know that without the investment of knowledge and experience of those ahead of me, my own journey will be far more arduous (and perhaps strewn with far more obstacles and mistakes) than would otherwise be necessary. I cannot give up or go backwards, and I do not want to continue to tread water, but I am not in a position to go forward with my dreams until I first gain the knowledge and experience I need.

I do believe that I am capable of gaining this knowledge, in spite of the fact that my previous academic record might appear to indicate otherwise. Before I share my dreams for the future, I would like to offer my perspective of my educational experience while a student at St. John's.

Grades. This is a tough subject to address. It's hard to know where to start. I don't want to gloss over this matter or treat it lightly. It is not easy to address because I want to be honest and objective and avoid giving lame excuses for being an average student, but I don't want to risk convincing you not to accept me for admission. In light of my past grades, you have reason to be concerned about whether or not I can be a successful graduate student. I myself have this concern. It is possible that I will not be a successful student, but I know that learning the coursework offered in your MPA program is crucial to the fulfillment of my dreams, so I cannot give up before even trying.

I have never been a straight-A, or even a straight-B student. In high school, I had a fairly predictable grade pattern. If I had to take a math or science class, you could expect a C in my transcript—at best. In English, French, Creative Writing, Humanities, Publications, and other literature classes, I normally did well (unless I overloaded on so many at one time that I couldn't keep up with them all, which was frequent). I usually earned B's in such courses, though a fair number of A's as well.

I went to St. John's College because the curriculum and method of teaching were exactly what I was looking for—almost. The concept was perfect. The curriculum was wonderful. In theory, I couldn't have asked for a better school to attend. That is, except for one little detail: me. I never seemed to find a way to peacefully coexist with math and science courses, nor come away from them with a decent grade. I absolutely loved St. John's and I wouldn't change anything but myself. I simply wasn't prepared for all the math and science with which I was confronted. I can balance a checkbook, but I have trouble with Einstein's Theory of Relativity.

I tend to be practical and concrete in my thinking, and have difficulty comprehending abstract concepts (especially mathematical and scientific concepts), a mental trait that never fit well with St. John's curriculum of philosophy, math, and science. I don't know why I am like this, or whether there is a cure for it, but I noticed this was a definite problem for me.

A lack of maturity and a lack of discipline also had a share of responsibility for my grades, but mostly...I lacked focus. At the time, I did not yet know where I was headed in life and I didn't know how to apply what I was learning to make it stick with me. I didn't have a foundation or a tether, and I didn't know what to do with everything I was learning. So, consequently, much of what I learned floated out into la-la land and never returned. (At least not yet.)

Another aspect of the program which was difficult for me was class participation. At the time, I was a very timid, shy creature. I was scared to death of my own shadow. It was sheer agony for me to even contemplate saying something out loud in class where everyone could hear me. I would steel myself up for an hour and a half just so I could blurt something out. My ears would ring loudly in my head, and my heart would race madly long after class was over, I was so scared.

I may not have exhausted the subject of grades, but at this point I would like to share with you my goals for the future. My whole life centers around a dream I have held since I was thirteen years old. I wanted to start an equestrian youth performing group similar to the Westernaires in Jefferson County, Colorado. I think the Westernaires group is wonderful, but not everyone is able to live in Jefferson County, Colorado. Westernaires needs to be like the Boy Scouts or Girl Scouts— a chapter in every city.

Ever since moving away from Jefferson County, I've wanted to take the Westernaires with me, but I couldn't. So I thought about starting my own group. At thirteen, the task was daunting. Way too hard. So for years I ignored it and tried to forget about it, but it never seemed to forget about me. It kept coming back to me. At the age of twenty-eight, I finally realized I couldn't let go of it. I felt called to it. So with blind faith and optimism, I set out to make it happen.

I had no idea what I was doing and I made countless stupid mistakes, but over the course of the last seven years I have also made some progress. I have learned a lot—the hard way. I have held horse camps and workshops for young people. I have had minor successes in fundraising and publicity. In July of 1993, after seven months of planning and a lot of hard work, I brought seventy members of the Westernaires (and forty of their horses) to Tulsa to perform the Horsecapades in order to demonstrate what I was trying to get started in Tulsa.

It may have been a very stupid idea, especially since I didn't know what I was doing, but somehow the show happened anyway. Over a thousand people attended, and hundreds of parents and children came up to me to tell me they wanted to be a part of it. The experience showed me that I was getting into dangerous territory. If I continued to pursue the dream— even in the haphazard, ignorant way that I had been—everything would get too big, too fast, while I was still trying to "wing it." I was convinced I would get myself into *big* trouble by not knowing what I was doing.

So, rather than continue and grow, I pulled back and tried to figure out how I could learn everything I needed to know, before I started to grow the organization. I have attended workshops on nonprofit topics, and read nonprofit magazines, but I finally realized that I needed to get some in-depth training and education from a program such as yours. So here I am.

I would like to add that after successful attainment of an MPA degree, I would like to attend Dallas Theological Seminary, or a similar school, and pursue an education in theology, because The Shepherd's Haven and The Equestrianaires are Christian ministries. I realize that I have not yet discussed my dreams for The Shepherd's Haven, and I could probably go on for pages and pages sharing my dreams and goals for that, but I realize how lengthy this letter is already, so I won't.

In closing, I know that my grades were mediocre. But I am no longer the same person I was. Now I have a purpose in life, a focus. I know where I am going. I am motivated, passionate, and enthusiastic. I know I can do this. I know that I will make mistakes, but I will learn from them. Everything that I learn from your program will have an immediate application; I will not waste any of it. I will use everything I learn to plan and implement the foundation of The Shepherd's Haven and The Equestrianaires. If you will accept my application for admission, and give me an opportunity to prove myself, I believe that I will be a credit to Drake University.

Please forgive me if this letter was too long. Thank you for your consideration.

Sincerely yours,

Kristin Kay Hoffman

I was accepted into the Master's Degree Program in Public Administration at Drake University and moved from Truth or Consequences, New Mexico, to Des Moines, Iowa. I began classes full time in August 1996. From January through May 1997, I was also given the opportunity to work as an intern for the State of Iowa House of Representatives, in particular, for Representatives Charles Larson and Rosemary Thomson. The experience was invaluable, enjoyable, and regrettably too short in duration. I enjoyed working with both of them immensely.

In most respects, it was a great year for my daughters and me. I studied for classes during the day while my daughters were in school, or worked as a House Intern, and attended evening classes four nights a week. Friday nights and weekends were ours to spend doing "girl stuff," watching movies, having sleepovers, and going camping. It was a time of reflection, a time to get my bearings and a time to heal. Did I have a call on my life or was I mistaken? What did I want to do with my life? What did God want me to do with my life? I had been knocked off-kilter, and was not following Him as closely as I had been, but I was trying to find my way back. I can only marvel, "Where would we be without God's grace?" Thank you, Lord.

Then I completed my degree program in August 1997 and returned briefly to Truth or Consequences, New Mexico, to stay with my mother while I decided which direction I was going to take next.

Chapter Six

STARTING OVER...AGAIN

When I returned to my mother's house in Truth or Consequences, New Mexico, I started looking for a job. Using Internet networking sites, I searched for jobs locally, statewide, in neighboring states, and then, randomly—*anywhere*. I couldn't seem to find a job that was right for me. I didn't want to stay in Truth or Consequences, but I didn't know where else to go. My mom had a house in Yalaha, Florida that was empty, but for some reason, she was having difficulty selling it. The idea occurred to me that perhaps the girls and I could move to Florida and live in her house. I could get a job and pay rent and it would help both of us out.

I don't know what it was that I was looking for, exactly, but I felt that something new was getting ready to happen in my life. I just didn't know what. As it turned out, the new "happening" in my life was not a new job, but a future husband, the love of my life. I met John Austin Johnson, of Hampton, Virginia, on the Internet, while searching for my next job. After that, everything started to happen very quickly. I can't explain *how* it all happened, it just *did*.

The long story short is that John came to New Mexico in October 1997, and together, we moved to my mom's vacant house in Yalaha, Florida. We were married on July 11, 1998. Heather and Katrina were eight and ten when we got married. I don't know what we were thinking. Think of *Yours, Mine, and Ours*, or *Cheaper by the Dozen*, minus ten kids, and you might come close to understanding the problems we faced. (Former Marine meets preteen *girls*.) Quite a few times in the early years of our marriage, it didn't look like we were going to make it as a family. I am so thankful that we did.

For the first couple years after moving to Florida, I worked in an administrative secretarial capacity in several jobs. In January 2000, I thought I might like to try being a teacher. So I called a high school principal just to ask what I had to do to *be* a teacher and ended up with a job interview on January 22. Okay, no problem. But then I was hired to *be* a 9th grade *math teacher*—starting on January 25.

My college transcript was loaded with math courses only because they were required curriculum. I was terrible at math. I thought it was a blessing when I was told that the schedules had been restructured so I would be teaching the three lowest level math classes. Okay, maybe that wouldn't be so bad after all. *Au contraire*. I had forty-five students in each of my classes—most of them ESOL (English speakers of other languages—though they didn't necessarily know a word of English yet). Others were ESE (Exceptional Student Education) and/or some other special group (like rival members of local gangs nobody warned me about). They showed me where my classroom was, gave me the keys, and that was it. So much for support. I didn't have a clue how to put together a grade book, much less a lesson plan. I tried to pretend I knew what I was doing, trying to learn the math lesson just ahead of the students, and the students just looked at me like I was their next meal. (Did I mention I hated math?) With several boxes of tissues behind me, somehow I survived the rest of the semester, *just barely*. Funny—the principal did not ask me to come back the next year. I was crushed by the rejection.

"I'm free! That's it. No more teaching. I tried it and it was not for me. So what do you want me to do now, Lord?" Never, ever, *ever* tell the Lord you are through with doing anything, and then ask Him what He wants you to do. *(Big mistake.)* His answer was a phone call

I received in July 2000. Yep, you guessed it. It was a phone call from another school principal who wanted me to interview for a teaching position for a new alternative school opening up in Bushnell, Florida, in August.

A dozen or so tissue boxes worth of tears wasn't enough for me, apparently, so I agreed to meet with her at a local bakery down the street from me. On July 10th, I walked away from the interview as the new math and English teacher for Excel Sumter Professional Academy in Bushnell, Florida. I would be teaching students in grades six through twelve. (Sounds just peachy, doesn't it?)

I didn't know much about how to be a regular teacher in a regular classroom with "regular" students, and I knew even less about how to work with the "difficult" ones—those who caused trouble all the time, had been expelled from their regular school, were in trouble with the law and had probation officers, were gang members, or had problems behaving "normally" because they had a history of abuse and neglect.

Over the next two-and-a-half years at Excel Sumter Professional Academy, the students taught me a lot about how to be a teacher, and about looking through all the labels, hurt, mistrust, and bad behavior to see them the way God sees them. I learned to love and respect my students, and most of them, I think, learned to love and respect me. After I left Excel, in January 2003, I spent another few years teaching in other schools. Yes, teaching math, ESE, Varying Exceptionalities— all the subjects I am so good at. (And people think that God does not have a sense of humor.)

Chapter Seven

CHINA: THE LAND OF THE YELLOW SEA BECKONS YOU

I have to give you a few details about how my daughters and I ended up teaching in China for the 2004 2005 school year. I had been teaching 7th and 8th grade math at Wildwood Middle School in Wildwood, Florida. I was teaching regular education and it felt like my first semester of teaching, all over again. By the end of the first semester, I started looking for something different to do because I was fairly certain I would not be returning the following school year.

For some reason (which I did not realize at the time was the Lord's prodding), I decided I needed to get passports for Heather and Katrina. So in April 2004, I sent in applications to get their passports. I had gone on a week-long mission trip to Honduras in March 2003, so I already had mine. At some point during the second semester, I started toying with the idea of getting a job as a teacher in a Christian school overseas.

I started sending out emails to principals at different Christian schools all over the world, literally. I was ready to go *anywhere*, even if it meant eating bugs and living in a mud hut in Africa. (Brave words, I know.) Believe me, I had no idea God meant to take them so literally. The school year ended, however, and I still did not have a job for the next school year. I continued to search on the Internet over the next month or so.

On the morning of July 4, as I scoured the Internet for job possibilities, I came across a website for teaching English in China. Not really thinking about what I was doing, I filled out a questionnaire about myself and my qualifications for teaching. Then I went to enjoy the rest of July 4th with my family. On July 6, at about 9:30 p.m., the phone rang. A voice with a thick Australian accent responded to my greeting. "Hello! This is Jeffrey Weymouth here, calling you from Beijing, China."

I am not sure, but I might have squealed in his ear. I was trying to get my husband's attention at the same time I was trying to keep the excitement out of my voice. I couldn't believe I had actually gotten a call from China. I am not even sure I had told my husband about filling out the application. As it turned out, Mr. Weymouth had to call me to hear how well I spoke English. The rest of my application was great—just what they were looking for, he said.

On Friday, July 9, I received an email from Mr. Weymouth's assistant, Miss Li Wang, congratulating me on being positively assessed and recommended for appointment to the Rizhao Juxian Middle School, which is an approved government school. I received a call from Mr. Weymouth later that same evening. He asked if I would be accepting the offer to teach at #3 Middle School in Rizhao, Shandong Province, China.

Earlier that day, my husband, John, and my daughters and I had discussed what it would mean to go to China as a family, and whether we should actually do it. I had always thought I wanted to be a missionary, but had never really considered I would have an opportunity to actually *be* one. The idea was a little bit scary for all of us, but we all decided that this was the opportunity of a lifetime and we should do it. So when I spoke to Mr. Weymouth, I told him we would be accepting the offer.

Over the rest of that month, my daughters and I had to get health certificates to send with our visa applications, book our flights, pack our belongings, and get ready for our journey. Everything happened so quickly that we realized we could not get everything taken care of before leaving, so my husband, John, stayed behind to take care of our house and pets. The original plan was for him to sell the house and then leave our cats with friends who would watch them for us. (We didn't think it would be a good idea to take them with us to China.) We thought he would be able to join us by Christmas. Unfortunately, we had no way of knowing that four hurricanes would strike Central Florida in quick succession that year—and one of them would take our roof with it. It took months to repair because contractors and roofing supplies were in high demand. So our house did not sell until June 2005, *after* the girls and I returned to Florida.

I will share here the highlights of our life in China as told through emails to our friends, pretty much the way that they were written. Some of our friends have given me permission to include here emails they wrote to us. (I have omitted email addresses and phone numbers, or otherwise obscured private information. I've shortened names to initials or first names only to protect the privacy of our acquaintances.) Also, just to warn you, the punctuation, grammar, spelling, and formatting tend to be even more "creative" in my emails than in my normal writing. (Rules, what rules?) So if you don't notice the creativity, bless my editor for cleaning it up, and commiserate with him for all the headaches he had to endure.

I will also include several emails we received from our Chinese friends during our stay in China, and even after we left. I include them here exactly the way they were received, leaving the content intact, including errors in grammar, punctuation, and/or spelling. They are precious to me just the way they are. They never fail to put a smile on my face. I tried writing a few of my emails to them in Pinyin Chinese, and I imagine I put more than a few smiles on their faces too.

-----Original Message-----
From: Kristin Johnson
Sent: Monday, August 16, 2004 10:10 AM
Subject: Just saying Hi!

Dear Mr. A.,

It has been quite a while since I last wrote to you, so I wanted to let you know what the Lord has worked out for me. He has opened a door and made all provision for me to go to Rizhao, China, to teach English at Rizhao Juxian Middle School this year! We leave for Beijing this Saturday. It has been pretty awesome—amazing—to watch the Lord at work this past month, making everything come together so smoothly and quickly. The Lord told me to just start walking toward the Red Sea, knowing that my feet would not leave dry ground. It was rather humorous when it dawned on me that rather than walking towards the Red Sea in faith, He really had in mind the Yellow Sea (literally) and just wasn't inclined to tell me just yet!

I wanted to share this with you because you were a part of my journey. You helped keep me on the path, and your correspondence was meaningful to me. (I hope I am making sense.) Anyway, if you would like to keep in touch or need to contact me for some reason, this email address will reach me in China. I just wanted to thank you again for the encouragement you gave to me when I needed it. May the Lord bless you and keep you.

In His grace,

Kristin Johnson

RE: Just saying Hi!
Monday, August 16, 2004 8:42 p.m.
From: Kristin Johnson
To: Mr. A.

Hi again,

I will be delighted to stay in touch and will let you know how things go for us in China. At this point, I don't know what the Lord has in mind as far as length of assignment. The initial contract is for two semesters. Anyway, as I keep in touch and the Lord lets me know what is going on, I'll be happy to share with you where He's leading me and for how long. Who knows, maybe someday it will be to Okinawa.

I will be praying for your school and that the Lord will abundantly provide for all your needs.

Blessings,

Kristin

We are here!

Sunday, August 29, 2004 7:16 AM
From: Kristin Johnson

Verdie,

We finally arrived at the school and I now have access to email. Please send me an email as soon as you read this so I will know you received it.

The girls and I are doing fine. It has been quite the adventure getting here. We spent one day in Beijing, and then they put us on a sleeper train at 10 p.m., Monday night. We didn't arrive in Rizhao until around 11:30 a.m. Three people from the school met us and took us to lunch at a fancy restaurant. Then they took us to have a quick look at the Yellow Sea before heading over to the school. I can't begin to describe the things we have seen here.

I have the phone number for our apartment. It is 00000000000. The girls and I bought cleaning supplies, towels, and food on Tuesday and spent most of the day cleaning our apartment and getting settled in. We also ate lunch with several officials at the school. It was an interesting experience to say the least. The people here are very friendly and concerned about our welfare. They are doing everything they can to make us feel at home and comfortable. They are trying to give us their best.

It is going to take some time to get used to the food here. They eat seafood in many of their meals—prepared in very strange ways. They literally use everything. When you eat fish soup, you get the whole fish: head, fins, insides—everything. It is the same with every other kind of meat they serve here. Most of it actually tastes pretty good once you get past the way it looks. We have also eaten many vegetables that we didn't know existed.

The other thing is that during special festive meals/ occasions, they drink a lot of Tsingtao beer. They served it to the girls and me, and had us participate in the toasts. During one round of several toasts, the girls very bravely swallowed about 6 oz. of beer (after looking to me for the OK).

This has been a real eye-opener for the girls. They have seen things neither they, nor I could ever have imagined, but overall, they like it here. This in spite of being convinced we are not going to survive if we have to spend much time walking or riding bikes on the streets. You wouldn't believe how crazy these people drive! New York streets are a piece of cake compared to braving these in China. Everyone disregards street signs and road markings. They constantly pass slower traffic, even into the path of oncoming cars, often missing head-on collisions with only centimeters to spare. You see every kind of vehicle you can imagine, from bicycles with two or three wheels with all manner of carts and box contraptions fastened on, to donkeys pulling carts on the streets as farmers bring produce to market. Animals literally walk the streets as they please—not just dogs—I mean cows and goats! We noticed this was especially common when we drove through a rural area. I'll write again later, and hope to catch you online sometime and IM you. Please write back soon.

Kristin

Life in China

Friday, September 10, 2004 7:51 AM
From: Kristin Johnson

Dear Wanda,

We arrived at the school nearly three weeks ago. Please send me an email as soon as you are able, so I will know you received this. The girls and I are doing fine. It has been QUITE the adventure getting here. After arriving around 5:30 a.m., we spent almost a full day in Beijing, walking around the famous Wan Fu Jing, or "Golden Street," and as far as one wall of the Forbidden City, but not the side with Tiananmen Square. After dinner, they put us on a sleeper train Monday night at 10 p.m., and we didn't arrive in Rizhao until around 11:30 a.m.

All our extremely bulky, heavy bags were piled up on my sleeper, so I was cramped up in one little corner, trying to sleep with my legs propped up on them. It was very uncomfortable. To make it worse, the sleeper across from me was empty most of the night, taunting me to come sleep on it, but a very sour, prune-faced woman kept coming into our compartment every few minutes to check and make sure I wasn't using it. The one time I tried to slip over to the empty sleeper, she came in, found me there, and gave me a vicious tongue-lashing in Chinese! So I resigned myself to very little sleep and a bad backache.

The next morning, three people from the school met us and took us to lunch at a fancy restaurant where we could see all the live fish and shellfish in tanks, waiting to be our next meal. We saw creatures we didn't know existed! After the meal, they took us to have a quick look at the Yellow Sea and then headed back to the school. I can't begin to describe the things we have seen here. The first afternoon, the girls and I bought food, cleaning supplies, and towels, and then spent most of the day cleaning our apartment and getting settled in. We also ate lunch with several officials at the school.

This has been a real eye-opener for the girls. They have seen things neither they, nor I could ever have imagined, but overall, they like it here. This in spite of being convinced we are not going to survive if we have to spend much time walking or riding bikes on the streets. You wouldn't believe how crazy these people drive! New York streets are a piece of cake compared to braving these in China. Everyone disregards street signs and road markings. They constantly pass slower traffic, even into the path of oncoming cars, often missing head-on collisions with only centimeters to spare. You see every kind of vehicle you can imagine, from bicycles with two or three wheels with all manner of carts and box contraptions fastened on, to donkeys pulling carts on the streets as farmers bring produce to market. Animals literally walk the streets as they please—not just dogs—I mean cows and goats! We noticed this was especially common when we drove through a rural area. I'll write again later, and hope to catch you online sometime and IM you. Please write back soon.

My classes are going very well. I only have to teach ten to twelve hours each week, but I have seventy to eighty students in each of my classes. The students are very respectful and well-behaved. They actually do what you tell them to do without complaining and with smiles on their faces! Well, I will let you go for now. I will be praying for all of you, that Hurricane Ivan will not bring more devastation upon you after Hurricane Frances made such a mess. I'll write again later. Please write back soon.

Kristin

Re: Update on China

Friday, September 10, 2004 7:31 AM
From: Kristin Johnson

Verdie,

Glad to hear from you again. I will definitely be praying for you, especially since Hurricane Ivan is heading your way, and also because of your husband's procedure the week of the 21st.

We are getting used to some of the food, mostly the vegetables. We are fast becoming vegetarians because the way they prepare meat is a little more than we can handle. My classes are going well. My students are mostly thirteen to fifteen years old, and for the most part, very well-behaved. I have seventy to eighty students in each of my classes, but I teach only ten to twelve hours per week. Such a deal!

The students are extremely respectful and obedient. They actually do what you tell them to do without complaining, and with smiles on their faces! It is so refreshing to experience such happy, contented students here.

Students are given a lot more freedom and trust here than in U.S. schools. They have ten minutes between classes, and instructors leave their classrooms to go to a break room to have a good rest between classes. No one worries about making sure they are in the classrooms and hallways, supervising students every second of the day. Students just do what they are supposed to do. Entire classes of students are left without an adult in the classroom to watch them. When you walk in, they are already doing exactly what they are supposed to be doing, quiet down immediately, and say, "Good morning, teacher!" It is so cool. I have not witnessed one disrespectful, smart-alecky act by any student (or anyone else, for that matter) since I've been here. They all treat one another with the utmost respect and dignity.

They treat the girls and me almost as if we are royalty. It is so cute how the women teachers love Heather's long, curly hair. They come up behind her frequently, begin stroking her hair, and say, "Oh, so very pretty! So very pretty." When we walk down the streets and go shopping, everyone stares at us and smiles. All the store clerks follow us around, wanting to get close to us and talk to us. It is almost comical.

Well, give my love to everyone at the school. I did try to send an email to Wanda at the school's address, so you might check and see if she got it and let me know. You are all free to share emails I send with anyone who is interested in knowing how I am doing. I will reply to anyone who sends me email. So far, so good. Love to all...Kristin

China Adventure

Sunday, October 3, 2004 11:03 AM
From: Kristin Johnson

Hey all,

It has been awhile since I last wrote, so here is an update on our adventure in China. I think that overall, the girls and I are enjoying many things about this experience. Of course, we all are homesick for family and friends, and we are suffering from culture shock, as most people do when they come to a foreign place, like China. For example, they do not place as high a priority on hygiene and cleanliness here, as we do in the States, so the girls and I often find ourselves in uncomfortable, miserable situations. Such as travelling as we have this past week and finding ourselves at the mercy of yucky, dirty, non-western restroom facilities (i.e. no toilets), with no options. (The girls thought they were going to die!) Also, the girls are now confirmed vegetarians for the duration of our stay in China, after seeing all manner of caged animals, mostly chickens, facing their untimely demise, being butchered right out there on the streets, and then sold. Within minutes, only piles of feathers and other debris are left to remind you they were there.

We have been gone quite a bit this past week. This past Tuesday, some Chinese friends took us to a mountain called OoWooGoo (spelling is approximate), where we spent a long, hard hour climbing to the top to reach a 1,000+ year-old temple, built for one of the Chinese kings (not sure which one). It was incredible to see, and we were glad we went. I didn't think I was going to make it to the top, but finally did. Turns out, I was just warming up for more climbing to come.

On Wednesday morning, one of the English teachers here took us by bus to go to Chufu, the birthplace and home of Confucius and several successive imperial officials and emperors, going back 2,500 years. It was incredible. We took zillions of pictures, so we will show them to you when we get back—maybe sooner, if I can get them developed and on disk somehow.

Then we went to TaiShan, or Mountain Tai, and spent the night. We got up before 5 a.m. to climb the mountain. We took a bus halfway up the 4,000 meters high mountain, and then got out to climb the rest of the way to the top on our own. What in the world was I thinking? When we looked up to see how far we had to climb, it looked as if the steps literally went all the way to the stars. I thought they would go on forever. I certainly did not think I would ever make it to the top. But I continued to climb, taking breaks every twenty to thirty steps or so. We climbed for three hours before reaching the top of the mountain at around 10:15 a.m. What a majestic, incredible view it was. It was magnificent. I hope our pictures will show even a portion of how awesomely beautiful the place was. After eating lunch and walking around the shops and temples at the top, we took a tramway back to the bottom of the mountain.

Once we reached the bottom, around 1 p.m., we took a taxi to the bus station, and then just waited and waited (and waited), until 4 p.m. to catch a bus back to the school. It turned out to be the bus ride from hell. The bus driver had been driving for over twenty-four hours and wanted to be relieved by another driver (so did I), so he kept driving for two hours from one bus station to another, trying to get the company to put a new driver on, but the bus company wouldn't do it.

Finally, he gave up and realized he was stuck with us...and we were stuck with him. So we left for Rizhao at 6 p.m., Thursday night. Though he was supposed to drive into Juxian first and drop us off before going to Rizhao, guess what? After a couple hours of driving, he decided he didn't feel like driving into Juxian, so he decided to drop us off at the highway exit to Juxian. He dropped us off at 9:30 p.m. or so (in the middle of the night). It was cold, pouring rain, and pitch black.

I was furious, to say the least, but it did us no good to complain. (Jenny argued with him furiously in Chinese, and he still kicked us to the curb!) Fortunately, before her cell phone lost service due to the bad weather, she had been able to reach her father and tell him what was happening, so he was already on his way to pick us up when we were dropped off. We walked in the driving rain to the toll booth exit, and her father showed up about five minutes later.

The next day, the Chinese family that took us to Oowoo-goo took us to Fulai Hill, another beautiful temple that featured the oldest gingko tree in the world. The tree was over 5,000 years old. There was also a small zoo there that was pathetic and sad. They had a couple of lions, a tiger, a couple of bears, ostriches, and an odd assortment of other animals in extremely small cages. My heart broke, just seeing them penned up in that manner. At least the ostriches were not caged up, but in a pen where they could run. After that, we climbed another mountain to the top. My legs were so sore by that time, I didn't think I ever wanted to see another set of stairs again.

Later that night, the same family took us over to their grandfather, aunt, and uncle's house, where we ate dinner with them, enjoying a delightful evening. We warmed up to each other almost immediately. They asked zillions of questions about America, and we learned a lot about China. They asked us to "please come back often" and also to "please come and enjoy the Chinese New Year" with them.

The holiday is over for us now, and I am back teaching again and enjoying my classes. We are slowly recuperating from the slight colds we got from walking in the rain and getting so cold.

Oh, also, I was on TV! When we went to Fulai Hill, some dignitaries happened to be there, and a TV crew was filming them. They walked up to me because it was unusual to see a "waiban" (foreigner) there. They asked me questions and why I was there.

Well, this update is turning into a novel, so I better quit for now. I will update you again soon.

Love to all, Kristin, Heather, and Katrina

China Update

Sunday, November 7, 2004 9:43 p.m.
From: Kristin Johnson

Hey everyone,

I am attaching an update I wrote in Word. It turned out to be another "novella," so please forgive me for that. I just had a great day yesterday and had a lot to share. I suspect I will have more great news to share with you again very soon, so I will follow it up in a short while.

Love to everyone,

Kristin, Heather, Katrina, and all the new and future saints in Juxian!

November 7, 2004

Greetings to all our family and friends,

It has been a while since I last wrote and gave you an update on how we are doing in China because not much seemed to be happening and I didn't have anything new to tell you. However, this has turned out to be an interesting week, with more than a few things to share. We would like everyone to pray for several people we've met. I will tell you as much as I can about each of them as we get to know them better.

There is so much to share, this may turn into another one of my "novellas," so please forgive me if it turns out to be fairly long. Also, I am typing as things come to mind, so hopefully, it will still make sense. This update is mostly about the people we have met and prayer needs for them. As to us—in a nutshell—the girls and I are doing great overall, except that they are extremely homesick. (Please pray that the Lord will help them get through this.)

The Tian Family

The family is made up of Mr. and Mrs. Tian, Sky, Summer, and Autumn (their English names), and a large assortment of aunts, uncles, nieces, nephews, grandpas, and grandmas. We have already met and shared meals and special occasions with most of them. They have been very warm and gracious to us, and have had us over on numerous occasions to spend the day with them. This is the family that took us to Oowoogoo (or Ooloogoo—can't remember which), the small mountain just outside of Juxian (not so small when you are climbing it), where we visited that 1,000+ year-old temple at the top. They also took us to Fulai Hill on October 1.

Last Sunday, they took us to a very fancy restaurant with many of their family members and we had the most delicious meal of our stay so far (although Mrs. Tian is an excellent cook and we always enjoy the meals she prepares). During the meal, they treated us as part of their family. Mr. Tian even told us that to them, we *are* a part of their family. The Tian family raises chickens and ducks and sell the eggs and/or the birds themselves. In the near future, they are going to build a large factory to increase production.

In a *casual* conversation, we mentioned celebrating Christmas a few weeks ago, and this past week, Mr. Tian told us that they wanted us to celebrate Christmas and New Year's with them. He even wanted to put up a large Christmas tree! We have been laying the groundwork and are praying that this will be an opening to share more about Jesus with them. Please pray for us.

Felicia

Felicia is a young kindergarten teacher who reads and speaks excellent English. A couple months ago, she walked up to us in the grocery store and asked us if she could help us with our shopping. She helped us carry our groceries all the way back to our apartment and has been coming over to visit us frequently ever since. She has been helping me to learn Chinese as well. She is precious. Yesterday, she took us to visit the kindergarten because she said her headmistress wanted to meet us. We went and spent over an hour with them. Little six-year-olds came up to us, speaking and singing nursery songs in English. It was too adorable for words. They asked us to please come back often to visit and we agreed that we would.

We planned to spend the day today with Felicia and two of my students who came to visit yesterday afternoon. They wanted to get to know the girls. They arrived early in the morning, as planned, and we left to go walking around, shopping, and to take photos. I discovered I had accidentally left the keys to our apartment on the hook on the wall inside and locked us out! Not good. I told the girls to go ahead with the others while I tried to find out how to get us back into our apartment. They all left, except Felicia, who chose to stay with me.

After informing school officials of what had happened, they sent some workers with us to see what needed to be done. It turned out this would be no easy task. We are on the second floor, and there are bars on all the windows, so getting through the door was our only option. It turned out, after a lot of frustration, and an odd assortment of tools (including a drill), they had to destroy the lock and kick in the door to get us in. While standing outside the door, I prayed to the Lord as myriad thoughts ran through my head.

I was feeling very aggravated with myself, asking how I could have been so stupid as to leave my keys in the apartment, when a thought flashed in my head: *There is a reason for this and it isn't stupid.* At first, I thought I was just talking to myself, trying to make myself feel better, making self-serving comments. But then the thought occurred to me that it could be the Lord speaking to me—at least I hoped it was.

Then, as I listened to Felicia singing to her, "You are my sunshine, my only sunshine," I told the Lord: "It is so sad that Felicia fell in love with a man who ended up marrying another woman, and now is heartbroken. She has no close family (something she had shared with us earlier). Lord, please save her and help her to find happiness." The thought quickly came back: *The man she was in love with was not the hus-band I have chosen for her. She will go to America and meet him there and you will help her get there. And yes, I will reveal myself to her. She is my child.*

Thinking they were my own crazy thoughts running rampant through my head, I tried to clarify and make sure it was the Lord talking to me and not me. But left up to me, I would not be charitable enough to offer to help someone go to America. I wouldn't dare to assume her husband would be waiting for her there. I wouldn't voluntarily put ridiculous, illogical thoughts like that in my own head because they made no sense. No sense at all.

So my conclusion is that either I am crazy, putting ridiculous thoughts in my own head that aren't true, or the Lord gave me a preview of what He was planning to work out for her. I am kind of excited, waiting to see what happens, even though it could end up being a long wait. Stay tuned.

A few minutes later, I asked the Lord: "Is Felicia the reason I locked my keys in the apartment? Am I supposed to tell her more about you today? Oh, and by the way, Lord, since they are having so much trouble getting the door open after working for over thirty minutes, can you send one of your angels to unlock the door like you did for Peter when he was in prison? I know nothing is too hard for you." A minute later, they got the door to open. The Lord answered and said: "No, I am keeping you home today for another reason. You will talk to Felicia, but not today."

A few minutes later, Felicia told me she needed to go home, so we said our goodbyes. Then I was left mulling over the thoughts that had been occurring to me. I was still sorting them out when my daughters and their friends came back and we spent some time visiting together.

Nikki

A few minutes later, the phone rang and I answered it. It was Nikki, a young woman who had called us over a month ago and told us she used to be friends with the foreign teacher that was here last year and she wanted to make friends with us. She teaches English at a technical vocational school up the street, just a block away. She came to visit us and we made friends, but we had not seen her since. She had been out of town for a month. She asked if she could come over to visit and I said, "Sure."

She arrived around 10:00 a.m., just as the girls and their two new friends were eating the brunch they had prepared. Nikki and I sat down and started talking about an English book she brought with her. She noticed some of the books we had that were in English and looked at them with interest and excitement. I showed her the girls' world history textbook. She said she liked history but could not remember much of what she had been taught in school. We looked at the chapters about China's history and she enlightened me on some facts missing from the textbook, though she said it was fairly accurate.

As we skimmed through many of the other chapters, we landed on the parts about the Middle East being the cradle of civilization and started talking about it. As we looked at the parts that mentioned the Hittites, Canaanites, Philistines, and others, I told her I had a book that was even better at explaining where these people came from and what they did. I pulled out the Bible and showed her the genealogy in Genesis that specified who was the father of whom; that Canaan was the father of so and so, and the father of Heth (the Hittites). For several hours, Nikki and I read through various portions and stories of the Bible, both Old and New Testament: the Flood, the Tower of Babel, Jesus, and more.

This all excited Nikki. She said she often listened to a radio station out of Hong Kong that talked about Jesus and played songs about Him. She wanted to know more about Him. We listened to several of my praise and worship CDs. She loved them—very much. Later, we found an online Bible website that had the Bible in the Chinese language. We read the first ten chapters of the Book of Matthew from it. We prayed together and Nikki took home my amplified Bible with her to read on her own. We talked about Jesus, read the Bible, and listened to praise and worship songs for almost eight hours before she left to go home. I told her she would have her own Bible in Chinese for Christmas, maybe before.

After she left, the Lord told me: "Nikki is the reason I kept you home today. She will be the first to come to believe in me, then Felicia, and then the Tians. I am building my body up around you in Juxian, and it will grow and prosper." As you can imagine, I am feeling absolutely euphoric right now. I am so very excited. So please pray for Nikki.

Well, I could go on, but I will spare you for a while. Things are HAPPENING here. Love to all in the name of Jesus.

We love you...

Kristin, Heather, Katrina, and all the new and future saints in Juxian!

-------------- Original message --------------

Hey everyone (again),

This is just a quick update to let you know that after praying for some time before Felicia came to our house tonight, the Lord gave me the words to share with her about Him as well as passages of Scripture He wanted me to share with her. It was a beautiful thing to watch. She got more and more excited as she listened and read as He revealed Himself to her. I could tell He was speaking to her heart and that she was listening to Him. I could see it written on her face (and God was telling me so as well). After a while, she indicated she wanted to be His child and have Him live in her heart. So we prayed and she gave her heart to the Lord, asking Him to live in her heart and be her Lord and Savior.

After she left, I called Nikki and she told me that she had started reading through the Bible from the beginning. She said she was going to read from it every night before she went to sleep. She wanted to come over to my house as much as possible so we can study the Bible together. (She will be coming over tomorrow.) She thanked me for sharing Jesus with her and said she was so very happy. I let her know that Felicia would be coming over to study the Bible with us as well and she was excited to hear this.

So anyway, now I am running out of Bibles. I have loaned out two of the three Bibles we brought with us. I know the Lord will provide them, but I am just sharing this need with you so that you can pray about it with us. If there were Bibles in Juxian, I would simply go and purchase them, but I don't think there are any in this city, and the girls and I are on foot for the most part.

Well, I wanted to share this praise report as quickly as I could.

Love to all,

Kristin, Heather, Katrina, Nikki, Felicia, and all the saints to come!

Lynn wrote:

Dear Kristin,

Your letters made my Monday! Sounds like we have a great new project for either our Sunday School class or our small group—Bibles in Chinese! Let us know how we can help get some in your hands.

Love,

Lynne

Re: Update to the Update on China

Wednesday, November 10, 2004 8:53 AM

From: Kristin Johnson

Dear Lynne,

I am glad that you all share my excitement. Both Felicia and Nikki came over last night, although they could not come at the same time. They both shared how extremely full of joy they were. They each shared with me the parts of the Bible they had read on their own, and we discussed the passages. I answered their questions as best I knew how. We prayed and listened to praise and worship music. It was a wonderful time of fellowship. They both plan to come over again Thursday evening for more Bible study, praise and worship, and prayer. My husband, John, is trying to get them over here as well, so you can coordinate things with him. He can share with you some of our conversations and concerns on this subject. Well, love to all in the name of Jesus.

Kristin

Kristin Johnson wrote:

Hey Verdie,

   I am getting ready for classes right now, but just wanted to send you a quick email. I have not heard from you in a long time, so wanted to check in with you. How is your husband doing? How are you holding up? I hope things are going better for you. When you get a chance, send me an email and let me know how things are going. Say hi to everyone at Wildwood for me. I hope you got the last email I sent—the novel, lol. Anyway, I hope to hear from you soon. I am praying for you and your husband.

Love, Kristin

verdie wrote:

Kris, glad to hear from you. I just got back last week. My husband is fine. He has to take it easy though. Keep praying for his strength. How are things going? Did you vote? How are the girls, hubby, the weather? Write back soon.

Verdie

Kristin Johnson wrote:

Hey Verdie,

   I was really glad to get your email and hear that you and your husband are both doing OK. Yes, I will be praying for your husband's strength to increase. Yes, I did vote and yes, things are going well here. If you read the last two updates I sent over the last couple days, you know that Nikki and Felicia have given their hearts to the Lord. We have been doing Bible study, praying, listening to praise and worship CDs, and praising the Lord.

It has been a very exciting week for me, and from what the Lord is telling me, it is going to be even more exciting with the passing of time. From this small, mustard seed beginning, He is going to grow and prosper the Church here. In a few years it will be large and vibrant. I look forward to seeing you when I get back home. Don't think for a minute that I have given up on our dreams for a school and all the things we have talked and prayed about. The Lord told me that those will come to pass, but He needed me to come here for a period of time to help His Church here in Juxian.

As I talked and prayed to Him last night, He told me I was an evangelist and that He planned to use me to start many churches, but that I (we) would still start our school and The Shepherd's Haven when the time was right (His time).

Well, I guess I will let you go for now. You should be in first period right about now. I am praying for you. Give my love to all our friends at Wildwood, and tell them I miss them (not the classroom grind, mind you, just them, lol). Take care of yourself.

Love,

Kristin

Verdie m.> wrote:

Kristin, glad you are successfully completing your mission for the Lord. We are thinking about carrying your legacy of the Young Explorers Club. Cody keeps asking Danielle, so we are thinking about starting the club. Everyone is fine. Continue to stay in touch, and may God bless your ministry richly. Oh, yes, when I pass the site where we prayed, I really think about how we were out in the rain, praying. My husband is ready to get back to normal. I am just as ready. Sometimes it is painful to me to watch him just put the best forward. Anyway, God is able.

Keep in touch.

Re: Have not heard from you in a while...

Thursday, November 11, 2004 9:13 AM
From: Kristin Johnson

Verdie,

I would be so excited if I knew that you were going to keep the Young Explorer's Club going, and to see it grow and allow the Lord an increased opportunity to work in the hearts and minds of the young students there. I often wonder how all of our students from last year are doing, especially the ones that got saved. If you hear from any of them, please let me know and give me an update on what is happening in their lives.

The Lord still intends to answer all of our prayers from the time we prayed in the rain, but the fullness of time has not yet come to fulfill them. When He moves to bring them about, it will not be a struggle for us to secure resources or anything else we need to carry them out. Just like when Moses brought the people out of Egypt, they did not leave empty-handed. They did not have to beg, borrow, or steal to get the things they needed. God will bless us abundantly and richly and we will have whatever we need. We will be a blessing to all the people in that area, not just Wildwood.

This is the year of the Lord's favor. Let us rejoice and be glad in it! Not to put a bug in your ear or anything, but check out the PlanetWisdom website, www.planetwisdom.com! Maybe you could take some of the kids to the conference again in January. I know it would be a huge undertaking, like it was last year, but last year was so awesome and the results were phenomenal. I think it would be awesome if it were to work out. The girls and I went to the 86 Hours Church Camp they had and it was so incredible. If we could get some of the Wildwood kids there, they would NEVER be the same. They would be sold out to Jesus and RADICALLY SAVED!

Well, anyway, feel free to give my email address to Danielle or whoever would like to write to me, and I will certainly write them back. Tell everyone I miss them and give them my love. Tell Wanda that I am praying for her and her brother, and would love to hear from her again when she has a chance. Oh, and while I was praying about your husband, the Lord told me he is going to be just fine and will regain his strength and then some. Just be patient a little while longer. Hang in there.

Love,

Kristin

Thursday, January 13, 2005 10:04 AM

Greetings to all of our family and friends,

It has been awhile since I last wrote to everyone, so I thought I would send you all an update on how we, as well as our new friends, are doing. I hope everyone enjoyed a wonderful Christmas and a safe New Year, albeit sad, because of the tsunami tragedy in the Indian Ocean and all the countries it impacted. It was especially sad to me because the people hardest hit by the tragedy were predominantly Muslim or other religions—not Christian. I was struck by how precious and fleeting life can be, and that we are not guaranteed time beyond the moment we have. The time to reach the world for Christ is now.

The girls and I celebrated Thanksgiving with Nikki, Felicia, and also the Tian family. With the Tian family, we talked about the things for which we were thankful to God and Jesus. We enjoyed the dinner with them very much. They expressed how much they were looking forward to celebrating Christmas with us.

The girls and I enjoyed a wonderful Christmas with several of our friends. When I got home from teaching my classes on Friday evening, Christmas Eve, I came home to discover that Mr. Yao, the dean of the school and the person who is directly responsible for the girls and me, had brought us a beautifully decorated, large Christmas tree and several gifts for us. He also told the girls that several of the school officials and teachers from the English Department would be taking us out to celebrate Christmas at a nice restaurant. We had a wonderful time. After dinner, we went back to our apartment. Nikki and Felicia came over and spent the night with us. We celebrated Christmas with them, and then watched a movie and snacked on popcorn and hot chocolate.

Later in the morning, before we left for the Tian family's home to celebrate Christmas with them, my Chinese doctor, Dr. Liu, came over, bringing us a beautiful flower arrangement for Christmas. Around noon, we went over to the Tians. They had put up a Christmas tree and were celebrating their first Christmas with us. After presenting them with their gifts, we relaxed and enjoyed the rest of the day, playing card games and watching movies on the DVD player we had gotten for them.

They served traditional Chinese festive dishes for the Christmas meal, and again later for dinner. I had brought a Chinese Bible with me, which I was able to show to Mrs. Tian. I was able to talk to her a little bit about it, and about Jesus.

The Tian family also picked us up on Monday evening and took us to a fancy restaurant to celebrate my birthday. They even got me a large birthday cake. They have been so very good to us. Please continue to pray for the Tian family, and us, as we continue to witness to them about the Lord.

The day after Christmas, two of my students and a brother of one of the students, Victor Wang (who is studying biology in a college in Jinan), came over to our apartment to visit with us. We had a delightful visit with them. Victor has been corresponding with us by email ever since. After mentioning Jesus to him, Victor expressed an interest in knowing more about Him. We have been exchanging emails about the Lord ever since. Please keep Victor in your prayers, that he will seek after the Lord with all his heart, and that He will find Him. I will keep you posted on developments with him.

On New Year's Eve, the school had a party in our honor. The local TV station in Juxian came out to film the event. So for a couple of days, everywhere we went, people told us they had seen us on TV. Then we went to Nikki's school and visited several classes of students, celebrating New Year's with them, before going to Felicia's kindergarten to attend a New Year's program there, which was excellent. Then Nikki and Felicia spent the night with us. We went to Nikki's home later in the day and ate dumplings, a traditional Chinese food.

On Sunday, Nikki, the girls, Dr. Liu, another doctor from his clinic, and I went out to a village in the country to the home of one of his patients, the Mung family. This family is in serious need of prayer. The father had been in the military for several years until he suffered a severe head injury, which has affected him mentally, rendering him unable to work. The mother suffers from high blood pressure and heart problems, so is also unable to work. Their seventeen-year-old son has a life-threatening disease, possibly leukemia, and is unable to attend school. The family does not have enough income to afford the cost of the boy's medicine or medical treatment of 450 yuan per month (1 Yuan = approximately twelve cents). I don't know how Dr. Liu is handling this financially, but suspect he is treating the family at his own expense.

For whatever reasons, the family is not receiving any assistance from the government (or anyone else, for that matter), except occasionally from other people in their village. The family lives in a small two-room mud and brick house which the villagers helped build for them recently. The house is not weatherproof. There are no beds or other furniture—not that the girls and I could see. They had no electricity. It was heartbreaking. We took huge sacks of flour, rice, cooking oil, apples, and oranges out to them and gave them money to help with medical and other expenses.

We told them that Shangdi (God) and Jesu (Jesus) love them very much and want them to know Him. They allowed us to pray for them. We told them as much about Jesus as we could before we had to leave. They asked us to please come back to visit them and we told them we would. They were very grateful. It was a very moving experience. Please pray for this family.

Dr. Liu and his brother are famous doctors here in China— wonderful people. We have become very good friends with them and been very blessed to get to know them. They have been helping me get my asthma under control and saved me from lung infections twice. (Typically, I get a lung infection at least once a year and have to treat it with antibiotics.) Dr. Liu prayed with us as we prayed with the family. He heard us tell the family about Jesus. He then took us for a nice lunch at a restaurant. Please pray for Dr. Liu, his brother, and his medical clinic. I can see the Lord using Dr. Liu and his brother in a mighty way, and am praying that they both will come to know Jesus as their personal Lord and Savior.

Nikki and Felicia are doing great, but they are so busy that we often see them only once during the week. They are both growing in the Lord and it is exciting to witness. They have both expressed a strong desire to serve the Lord and are seeking Him with all their hearts. Please continue to pray for both of them. Hopefully, during the Winter Holiday, which begins in another week or so, we will be able to spend more time with them, and perhaps visit some churches in other cities such as Qingdao, Nanjing, or Jinan. If you would like, you can email Nikki. I know she would be very excited to get them. When Felicia gets an email address, I will give you hers as well.

I have been put in contact with Chinese pastors here through the Outreach Foundation, and have been corresponding with them through email, which has been wonderful. I am looking forward to an opportunity to personally meet as many of them as I am able to before we leave here. Please pray for the Church and pastors here in China.

Well, there are several more people I could tell you about, but I think I will save that for a future update. We miss everyone very much and often think about you all. Thank you for all your prayers and concern.

Blessings,

Kristin, Heather, and Katrina

Mike wrote:

Hey Stargazer!

I talked with John last night. I finally have email access again, after being computerless for some months. I was delighted to hear that your pastor is my old buddy, John L. We were in seminary together, next door neighbors, in fact. The first churches we served in Ohio were only a few miles apart, so I spent a lot of time with him, Mary, and the kids. Sarah was just a baby then. Now, I understand, she has twins of her own. Rachel wasn't even born yet. I met her later.

How are things in China? I missed calling you on your birthday a few weeks ago (I haven't forgotten). I think of you often and cherish our friendship, KK. Know that you are in my thoughts and prayers. Greetings to Heather and Katrina, too.

Much love always,

Mike

Hey Mike,

It is great to hear from you. We have been trying to get back in contact with you ever since we discovered that you and John are friends. Somehow, John didn't get your new contact information the last time you called him, so the only thing I had was your email address, which I was unsure was still valid. We are so glad you called back after John located your new church, and called and left the message for you.

The girls and I are doing great here in China, although we are getting homesick for friends and family back home. I am attaching the last few updates I sent to everyone since we have been here. You are on my email list, so you will get them from now on. I hope everything is going well for you, your wife, kids, and grandkids.

Looking forward to hearing from you again.

Love, Kristin

Another China Update

Friday, April 22, 2005 9:37 AM

From: Kristin Johnson

Hey everyone,

The other night, my husband, John, *gently* reminded me that it had been quite some time since I wrote an update to let you know how we are doing, and to "get busy." Since I last wrote to you all, the girls and I have enjoyed the Spring Festival and Lantern Festival, which were very loud, boisterous holidays, filled with fireworks, lights, and candles, that didn't seem to have a specific beginning or end. The girls and I were serenaded with fireworks at all hours of the day and night for several weeks during the month-long school break. Everyone was in a festive mood. It was fun!

We also managed to go to Qingdao for a few days on two separate occasions and visited two different churches there. We met several Chinese Christians and it was a heart-warming experience to say the least. We have also been to Rizhao a couple times and met several of Nikki's classmates and friends. The girls filmed a rather comical "documentary" of several portions of these visits for your viewing pleasure, including the afternoon when we visited the Laoshan Temple in Qingdao.

Rather than allowing ourselves to be taken advantage of by the taxi drivers and pay triple fare for the sixteen kilometer ride back down the mountain, my indignant pride caused us to choose to walk away and begin the arduous trek on foot. The Lord was merciful to us, however, sending along an angel of mercy in a garbage, err, "cargo-laden" truck about twenty minutes later who stopped to pick us up. Nikki found a perch in the back of the truck, atop some interesting treasure, while Heather, Katrina, and I squeezed into the space of one passenger in the front seat. My knee rubbed against the gearshift most of the way down the mountain. Heather captured it on film, so you can share the experience with us when we get home.

As it happens, we discovered there is a church here in Juxian, and started attending services there a couple weeks ago. The pastor is Mr. Yu, a very warm, friendly man (as you would expect). He has an equally friendly wife and adorable small daughter. We have also met several people who attend the church. They can be most easily described as precious. Because of the language barrier, it has been difficult to learn their names, personal histories and such. But it has been an amazing experience, worshipping with them and feeling the Holy Spirit's presence among us (even though the girls and I couldn't understand a word that was said).

The girls and I will undoubtedly share more detailed accounts of the activities and things we have experienced over the past couple of months, but I am trying to type things as I think of them, to cover them before I forget. We have taken dozens of pictures to share with you. I introduced Pastor Yu to Dr. Liu. I showed Dr. Liu the *Jesus* film, which made a strong impression on him. This Sunday, Dr. Liu is planning to attend church with us.

Last week, the seventeen-year-old Mung boy (we named him "Joseph") came into town to register at a technical vocational school—something Nikki had been able to get approved by her school. We all went to the school—including Dr. Liu—and got Joseph registered. I even paid his tuition for the first semester. Then we took him to a market and bought him a few new shirts, a pair of pants, jacket, socks, and a pair of tennis shoes so he would have some appropriate school clothes to wear to school. I also gave him a Bible as a gift.

Today Joseph and his mother came into town for his first day of school. Dr. Liu came to pick us up and brought a TV reporter to record the event, something I had not expected. Anyway, the girls and I went to the school with Dr. Liu and the TV reporter, where Joseph and his mother were already waiting. Pastor Yu was there as well, because I had asked him to come and talk to Mrs. Mung and tell her more about Jesus if the opportunity presented itself. We paid all the final fees for Joseph's books, meal card, uniform, and more. Then we helped Joseph get set up in his dorm room.

At lunch time, we went to eat at a restaurant nearby. Joseph and his mother were unable to join us, so we left them at the school. After lunch, Nikki had to go back to work at the school. The girls and I went back to the church with Dr. Liu and the pastor. They visited with each other for quite some time. We couldn't understand anything they were saying except for a few words every now and then. From the few words I did understand, I could tell the pastor was talking to Dr. Liu about Jesus. We didn't get home until almost five that afternoon.

The girls and I are down to our last ten weeks or so of being here in China. It has been a really awesome experience in so many ways. Right now, we are planning to take a week or so during the May holiday and travel through the South of China. That is assuming, of course, that the school actually gives us the week off—just like everyone else in China gets. They haven't told us yet, for sure, so we can't make concrete plans. If we do get to go, we will be taking Nikki with us. Felicia will not be able to go because she needs to go back to her home village to visit her parents. She is doing great, by the way, but has been so busy we have not seen her very much lately, although she did go to church with us last Sunday.

In other interesting news, Nikki met Joshua (supposedly by "accident") only a few weeks ago. Sparks flew! He was completely smitten with her, immediately informing her parents that he would like to be engaged to her and marry her when he returns in three years and retires from the army. Despite her earlier comments (pre-Joshua), that she wasn't sure she wanted to get married, after meeting Joshua, it was obvious her heart had changed her opinion on the matter. (She had, in fact, ignored several previous opportunities to get married.)

Needless to say, it has been very cute to watch the two of them together. Joshua only has eyes for Nikki, and Nikki glows. She also blushes when we tease her about all the text messages he sent her at all hours of the night while we were in Rizhao. You might be thinking that all of this happened very quickly, but marriage customs in China are very different...and interesting. The use of matchmakers is common, and arranged marriages still occur, to an extent. The concept of love doesn't always hold a high priority in the marriage decision.

Before I forget, the Tian family is doing great as well. They succeeded in getting their chicken factory built and it officially

opens on May 1st. It will employ well over one hundred people. I introduced Mr. Tian to Pastor Yu and they had a friendly
visit, but Mr. Tian told Pastor Yu that he never has time to go
to church. Keep praying for him. Sky and Summer, however,
plan to attend church with us this Sunday. There are several
other activities and things I could tell you about, but then this
really would turn out to be a book (and I have tried very hard
to keep things brief in this email).

I have already begun my quest for a teaching position or
other job once I return to the States, so I would be grateful
for all prayers in this regard. Okay, I will close this so I can get
it sent. We love you all and miss everyone. We shall see you
soon.

Love,

Kristin, Heather, and Katrina

RunShengTang

Thursday, August 18, 2005 2:05 AM
From: RunShengTang
To: "克里斯婷" Kristin Johnson
亲爱的朋友：
您好！

Dear Mrs Kristin

I fristly wish all your families being happyful and healthy,
and all best wishes to you.

Time flies, and it has been two months since we sent you off
in Beijing. Everyone at Runshengtang clinic miss you very very
much in these two months. I didn't get touch with you in time
because of our different languages, and I beg your forgiveness.

We have read the email sent buy you carefully. I know that you have started a new proper job, and Heather and Katrina have gone to school, too. Congraulation! We are also very glad for your planting to build a church here. When we sent you off on June 18, 2005, at Beijing International Airport, we saw your backs until you walked further and father and disappeared from our slight in the end.

Although we apparently had no tears that day, we were awefully sad in the bottom of our hearts. We visited for about 30 minutes at the airport just waiting to say goodbye to you, but you didn't come out. We knew that it would take a long time for you to finish the check because there were so much passengers. Also, there was a long distance between the airport and the bus station and we must get on our bus at 8 o'clock in the evening in order to return Juxian. Therefore, we lost the chance to say goodbye to you. What a pity, however, it may be the best.

You are my best American friends. I will remember and miss you forever, and I believe that we will meet again in the near future. With the rapid development of modern science and technology, we are able to express our feelings by email. In a word, we miss you very, very much. Hopefully our true friendship will last forever and be remembered by heart.

Wish your families being happyful again.

All the best wishes to you , and happy every day

致礼！Liu Liancheng

August, 18th, 2005

RunShengTang wrote:_

Hello:

   __Can know you , we are very glad to be very honoured__
__too ~~!__

   __A long time meet, we extraordinary miss you. How is__
__your life now? Have missed us? Oh ~~~! !__

   __Has time been given your wishing you to receive a bit__
__ago? The new year is coming, wish you are during the new__
__year: The health work is happy! !__

   __Grow the hall in five generations traditional chinese__
__medical science clinic moistly . China__

Re: run sheng tang

Sunday, January 1, 2006 6:52 p.m.
From: Kristin Johnson
To: RunShengTang

Dr. Liu,

   Xie Xie. Xin Nian Kuaile! Heather, Katrina, and I miss you
all very much. Thank you for the Christmas and New Year's
cards. We think about you every day and miss you all. Someday we will come back to Juxian and see you again. We will
never forget any of you or the many happy times we shared
with you. We love you all very much. I sent a letter to Nikki
and asked her to send our love to you. We will keep in touch
with you often.

   Heather and Katrina are in school and I am teaching in a
middle school. We are doing very well. We will continue to

pray for the happiness and well-being of you all. You are in our hearts forever, and we are family. Please tell everyone you see who know us that we love and miss them too, especially the boy and his family.

Love to all, Kristin, Heather, Katrina, and John

Re: How are you?

Thursday, October 30, 2008 8:36 p.m.
From: "Kristin Johnson" <kristikayjohnson@yahoo.com>
To: "于娟" nikkiyu >

Nikki,

I was so happy to hear from you. I think about you all the time, but I have been so busy that I never have the chance to call you. When there are good times for me to call you, they are the wrong time for you because I would be calling in the middle of the night! We certainly do miss you.

I am so happy to hear about your new job. I hope it is a really good job for you and that you will be happy in it. How are your husband, Wen Ji, your parents, and all your brothers, sisters, nieces, and others? What about your mom and father-in-law who both have heart conditions? Are they doing okay? Quite often, my church lifts all of you up in prayer.

How is Dr. Liu? Do you still get chances to see him? How is Joseph? When you get a chance, write me back and tell me how everyone is doing. Please, when you see anyone we know, let them know we still think about them, love them, and miss them. Money and time have made it difficult for us to return to China, but someday we would love to go back. I hope to bring my husband back with me one day. Also, my dream would be for you to visit America with your husband

and son. Do you still have the same phone number? If it is the same, I will try to give you a call soon. If not, email me your new phone number and try to email me more often. I will do the same. WE MISS YOU.

Send Heather and Katrina an email. I know they would love to hear from you!

Love, Kristin

From: 于娟 nikkiyu >
To: kristikayjohnson@yahoo.com
Sent: Thursday, October 30, 2008 4:11:49 AM
Subject: How are you

Hi Kristin,

I changed my work one week ago. Now I am working in a home textile company in Juxian. My main work is dealing with exporting affairs. Our company mainly exports beddings. I find sorts of beautiful fabrics, fake flowers and other decorations that can be used to make beautiful dress, which often makes me think of Katrina. She must be very intrested in the fabrics. When will Katrina graduate? If she has time and chance, she is welcome to our company. May I have Katrina's E-mail address or she can send me E-mail if she is intrested. I will go to Guangzhong with my manager and colleagues from Novermber 1th to 7th to attend trade fair.

Miss you and best wishes,

Nikki

I have corresponded with Nikki through postal mail and email since we left China. Over the years, friends we made in China have sent us updates on events in their lives. Most of it is happy news, but some of it is very sad. After receiving a lot of happy news about Joseph completing school and going to various cities to work as a tailor, we were saddened to learn from Nikki a few years ago that she had received a call from Joseph's mother to say he had passed away as a result of his illness. Joseph and his family meant a lot to us and it makes me sad that he is gone.

Dr. Liu is apparently doing well and his clinic is more famous than ever. It has been a while since I last corresponded with him, but every once in a while I still get a Christmas or New Year's Eve card from him. I plan to send him an email to see how he is doing. I will post an update on his status when I do.

Nikki married Joshua soon after we left. Within a year, she had a son, Wen Ji. I have received Christmas cards from her, and even received a handwritten Christmas greeting from Wen Ji this past Christmas. He told me he plans to come visit his American Aunt (me) in America when he gets older. I would be so delighted and excited for that to happen. Can't wait. I really miss Nikki and Felicia. They mean so much to us, even after all these years of separation. We love them.

I chatted with Nikki a couple of nights ago through Yahoo Chat and she told me she had been to church with Felicia. She said Felicia loves going to church and being a Christian. It had been a long time since I last talked to Nikki, and until our chat, we had not talked too much about Felicia. I don't really know the dates and times of some of the events Nikki told me about, but I know that Felicia met and fell in love with a man not long after my daughters and I left China. I do not know his name or anything about him, but I learned from Nikki that Felicia now has a beautiful daughter, Yan Yan, who is four years old.

Yeah, I know, I got that one really wrong. I thought she was coming to America to meet her husband. Even so, I pray that Felicia will bring her family and come to America some day. I would be so thrilled to show them our country.

Chapter Eight

RETURNING HOME FROM THE YELLOW SEA

We returned from Beijing, China, on June 18, 2005, Heather's 16th birthday—which we celebrated twice. We celebrated it first in China and then on the next day, in Los Angeles, California. Such a deal.

As it happened, our house sold a week or so after we got home. We spent the next month or so living in our recreational vehicle until we bought a new house to live in. At the end of July, I went to a job fair, looking for a secretarial job. Yep, you guessed it. I left with another teaching job. I would be working as a math teacher for SED children, grades six through twelve, for Life Stream Academy in Eustis, Florida. (SED stands for severely emotionally disturbed.) I taught at Life Stream for the next year-and-a-half.

October 2006

For some time, I had not been feeling particularly confident in my role as a special education teacher, working with emotionally disturbed teenagers. This, coupled with severe family conflict we struggled with at the time, left me feeling anxious, out of sorts, and bewildered. It finally dawned on me that I had been worrying more than praying (and even then, only half-heartedly). I had shut the Lord out and was not asking Him for help, insight, or guidance. I was afraid of what He would tell me.

I don't recall if I initiated the conversation or if the Lord did, but I spent an entire sleepless night in prayer, pouring my heart out to Him. I asked Him if I was doing what I was supposed to do or completely off track, and if so, what I was supposed to be doing. I asked Him to help me get back on track and be the person He had called me to be. It was then that the Lord reminded me He was in charge of my life and that He was not through with me yet. He told me to quit complaining about my age and infirmities, and to stop giving Him every excuse in the Bible (as He had already heard them all). He challenged me to read the stories of Sarah, Abraham, and Moses, and to then try and tell Him I was too old, decrepit, or sinful for *anything* He asked me to do. At that point, I decided it would be a good idea to shut up. He had given me the dream of The Shepherd's Haven years before, and it was time to get started—not the time to hold back because I felt small, unworthy, and insignificant.

Chapter Nine

THE MESSAGE

I was still talking to God the following morning in my classroom, during my planning time. It was October 13, 2006, when He instructed me to get pen and paper and start writing down what He was telling me. I expected that His words would be a personal message to me, concerning my life and current situation. I began to write down the words that entered my mind, which came almost too quickly for me to keep up. It was only later, when I actually read the message I had written, that I noticed that only parts of the message were directed to me, individually. More often, God directed the message to "each of you," a group of people, the identities of which, as yet, only He was aware. I know it is a little confusing, but God knew He was addressing His message to multiple people, even if I did not realize it, so I leave the message as He gave it to me.

I don't know how to untangle the message to separate the parts that were only intended for me from the parts of the message He intended to be for everyone else. The message references the Greek classes I took for two years in college, which might not be applicable to you, however, He was simply rephrasing and expounding upon John 1:1, and its sentiment applies to everyone. If the message speaks to your heart, and you get the feeling that God is directing these words to you and you "know who you are," then God gave me this message to share with you.

In this message, God made numerous allusions to prophets, books, terms, and events in the Bible with which I was not overly familiar, especially those from the Old Testament. It caused me to go look them up. To that point, I had not been particularly faithful in reading the books of the Bible, especially Deuteronomy, Leviticus, and similar books. So I had to spend a lot of time reading the Bible myself, just to understand what He was telling me. God instructed me to record the date and time that these messages were given to me. I did not understand the reason for this until many years later. The message He gave me I now share with you:

10/13/2006
9 a.m.

I am the Boss. I am the Head. I make the decisions. Through prayer, you WILL hear my voice, I will make it *plain*. I will make this happen; I will bring it about. I will accomplish it, for it is my dream, my vision, my purpose I have given to each of you. I have called you to perform it together. Do not hinder one another. You are the army of Joel. You will look neither to the right nor to the left but straight ahead at the task I have set before you. You will do what I have called you to do.

Do not worry about money. All the money in the world is under my control. Listen to my instructions and be careful to follow them. Do not lag behind nor try to run ahead. I will go before you and come behind you—I will encompass you. I am your retirement—your exceedingly great reward. Read Deuteronomy 28. Believe it. Trust me. Am I a man that I should lie?

You are where you are right now because I led you there. You are following my plans and purposes for your life. Don't worry about hearing my voice and missing something. I can and will use anything I need to in order to make my voice heard by you—to make my wishes known to you. Don't worry about people who try to come against you. It is not a wise thing for anyone to set themselves up against my children, my anointed servants. Those who do this set themselves up against me, and I will surely deal with them according to their deeds.

Many people will serve as "lessons" in your life. You must all remember (and learn this well), that many people under your authority are serving me just as you are. Don't hinder them; empower them. Build them up. You would do well to never forget this.

Each of you, write the vision down that I have given you, make it plain. I will accomplish it. I will perform it.

10/13/2006
9:30 a.m.

Write down everything I tell you. Record it and follow it.

Be prepared. I am on the move and I will begin to send people to you, or I will send you to them. They will be ready to receive you, just as you will be ready to receive them. When they come, you will know that I have sent them.

Be prepared for the windfall. I will provide you with everything you need, *when* you need it.

Your first book will provide resources for the ranch property and I will use the book to draw the people who will come to build it. Remember Nehemiah? Is anything too hard for me?

Treat my people well. My servants—my children—are worthy of their hire. Pay them well. There will be bread in my house and NO ONE who comes to me will be hungry or thirsty.

Doctrine? Don't worry about doctrine, denominational differences, and such. If you find it in my Word (for it *is* my Word), trust it and do it. Don't waste your time arguing about it with anyone. It is simple: *Feed* my sheep. Love one another as you love yourself. If I am lifted up, I will draw all men unto *me*.

I have given the dream—the vision—to each of you. Many of you have been waiting and looking for its fulfillment for years now. As each of you begins to write down the vision you have been given, you will marvel at how similar they are. You will see the similarities and realize that it has been given to you, by me. It is from me. Your dreams and visions are my dreams and visions. They *are* one and the same. When my Word goes forth it shall NOT return to me void. It will be filled with purpose and shall accomplish everything for which I sent it.

In the beginning was the Word, and the Word was with God and the **Word** *was* God. I *was* (and am) **the Word**. I create with nothing more than **my Word**. I *need* nothing more. I spoke this world into existence. Everything that you see—and billions of things you haven't seen or even dreamed of—came into existence at MY WORD.

I speak into existence worlds and universes, yet sometimes you are afraid to trust ME. I feed and clothe the small, unseen creatures you know nothing about. I know your every thought and have numbered every hair on your head. I save your tears when you cry. Yet you have a hard time believing MY WORD—trusting that I can do BIG THINGS for you and in your life.

Yes, the vision will require a lot of money, land, and people. I know this is scary for you to think about. You have held back from starting because you feel so small, unworthy, and insignificant, doubting I would choose you and not others for this. I say, why **NOT** YOU? I have called you by name—years ago. I gave you the DREAM and you heard me (you know you heard me). Do not be like Jonah. Do NOT run away from this! Do not be like Jeremiah or Moses and give ME excuses.

I will provide everything you lack as you need it. I will be the pillar of cloud by day and the pillar of fire by night. Giants you face are not even grasshoppers to me. I laugh at them. I still sit on my throne and laugh. The nations may rage against me and come against my holy city, but they shall not prevail. My will and my Word shall NOT BE TRAMPLED UNDER. They shall stand and not be moved.

10/13/2006
2:05 p.m.

Remember what I spoke to you all those years ago. Write it again and hold to it. Remember it!

Many people will see the need to have this place for the children. As I move to bring MY PEOPLE back to me, to renew and restore their love for me, I will provide a place for ALL to come to me. I will accomplish it. For I have spoken and my Word shall go forth and accomplish my will and purpose. It only takes ONE PERSON, listening prayerfully and obediently to Me, to provide the money for the purchase of the property. (This part was originally spoken to Phyllis Hicks sometime in August 1989, soon after I shared with her the dreams God had given me, and we prayed about The Shepherd's Haven. I lost touch with Phyllis years ago, and have been unable to locate her. So Phyllis, when you read this; CALL ME!)

Those of you I have spoken to—and you know who you are—commit and set aside time to pray together diligently and earnestly for the vision to come to pass. As I provide guidance and direction, OPENING DOORS, AVENUES, and HIGHWAYS, be SURE to step out in faith and follow me. Do you have faith even as small as a mustard seed? If so, watch it grow and bloom and flourish—even as the cedars of Lebanon. Trust me. Watch and walk in faith. You are a story in the Bible. You are writing it NOW. What will it say? Will it say that you believed me? Yes! You will walk in faith. Believe in me—my Word is truth.

At the time I was uncertain as to whether the message was actually from Him or only the longings of my own heart, so I filed it away among other keepsakes and eventually forgot about it, only retrieving it years later when He reminded me of it. But you now have some idea of why I am publishing this book. I was told to write the vision down and to make it plain. There is some repetition in this book because many times, when I asked the Lord a question, He would give me the same answer, which was already in the message He had given me. The repetition bothered me, so I asked the Lord what to do about it. He told me, "Repetition is good. How many pages are in the Bible?"

"Hmm, about 1,500 pages, give or take a few, depending on whether you count the index and stuff—and how large the type is," I replied.

"How many prophets did I have to send to the same stiff-necked, rebellious people over and over, to tell them to repent and obey me?"

"If you want a quick answer on that, was it forty, maybe? I don't know. I would have to read it through and count them, which might take a while."

"This is important. My message is short and simple but it still took 1,500 years and 1,500 pages to get my point across and still, my people do not get the message. I want them to GET THIS MESSAGE."

Chapter Ten

A JOURNEY ABROAD

In November 2006, I left Lifestream to teach at another middle school. After that, I switched to teaching an EBD (Emotionally Behaviorally Disturbed) exceptional student education class at the elementary level at Orlo Vista Elementary School in Orlando, Florida in April 2007. (Don't you just love those labels—SED, EBD, and so on?) It wasn't so much that I forgot about the message, I just didn't know what to do with it. I was overwhelmed with learning how to teach younger, special needs children, so trying to become an excellent teacher became my focus for the next couple of years.

During the summer of 2008, I had an opportunity to teach English for Swiss Village Camps in Cork, Ireland for four weeks. I also had the opportunity to do some additional traveling for three weeks throughout France, Italy, Austria, and Switzerland. My husband, John, was able to join me for the last week I was in Europe and we were able to visit Rome and Venice, Italy, Salzburg, Austria, and Zurich, Switzerland. (So romantic.) The following email is about some of the experiences I had during my travels before, and during the time I worked at the summer camp.

Adventures in Europe

Tuesday, July 8, 2008 1:03 p.m.
From: Kristin Johnson

Hi everyone,

It has been a while since I last sent an email and updated you on my general whereabouts and travels. After spending a few days in Paris when I first arrived, I took a night train to Vicenza, Italy, where I was met by my friend, Stellina, the next morning. After spending a wonderful, relaxing morning visiting with Stellina, she took me to Venice that afternoon and we spent several hours walking around the streets and over canal bridges, touring all the famous buildings, palaces, and squares in Venice. I took a lot of pictures and will try to send a few now. (I will also be happy to show them when I get back.)

Stellina took me around to various places in and close by Vicenza, telling me all about its fascinating history. We spent one evening at the home of another friend of hers, Laura, and the three of us went to a restaurant and ordered a REAL Italian pizza that was delicious. The pizza ovens they use are far different from what we have in America. Stellina took pictures for me to show you how they work, but I will have to send them at a later date, because I haven't gotten them from her yet. Basically, it is a huge cylindrical stone (approximately 6 feet in diameter) that rotates around as fire at one side provides heat to all the pizzas.

After making the pizza, they use a long-handled, flat, shovel-looking thing (can't think what it's called) to slide the pizza directly onto the stone surface. Well anyway, after spending a few days with Stellina, I needed to start heading for Ireland. So I boarded a train and went to Zurich, Switzerland, and spent the night at a hostel. The next morning I took another train back to Paris and then transferred to a different train to Cherbourg, France. From there, I planned to take a ferry to Rosslare, Ireland.

Unfortunately, the train had some mechanical problems and was delayed getting in to Cherbourg. I lugged my bags (five of them—each easily 50 lbs.) the mile-and-a-half or so from the train station to the ferry station. (Ugh! Not fun at all!) By the time I finally got there, I had missed the last ferry by about 30 minutes. It was Thursday evening, there would not be another ferry leaving for Rosslare, Ireland until Monday, and I was supposed to be at the Camp by Sunday. (Not good.) It turns out I had to get to Roscoff, France in order to catch the next ferry that would leave there Saturday night at 6:30 p.m.

I spent the night in Cherbourg at a rather expensive hotel (not worth the money I paid, but everything else was booked and I was desperate). The next afternoon, I set out for Roscoff by train. I spent Friday night in Roscoff. I walked around town the next day and finally walked over to the ferry station to depart for Ireland that evening.

The ferry trip over was actually pretty cool, in more ways than one. "Frozen" might be a better word to describe it. Trying to save money (being cheap), I didn't book a cabin with a bed, only a seat. I would have to sleep sitting up all night. I had my travel pillow and a very thin blanket to keep me warm, but I still froze to death most of the night. The armrests were not adjustable, so though the seats around me were empty, I still could not put them up and stretch out across the seats.

I woke up several times during the night, half asleep, with a massive crick in my neck. I was stiff and sore all over. Other than that, it was actually fun. There were a couple of birds that took the ferry with us. They perched atop the emergency boats and stayed there for the longest time before deciding they were rested enough to continue their journey under their own wing power.

The next day, I took the train to Cork, Ireland, and was met by the camp director. The camp was still being set up and the camp director and some of his regular staff were busily traveling from airport to bus station to train station, collecting all the camp counselors as they arrived. Later that night, we all got together for our first staff orientation meeting. We ate pizza and had the opportunity to visit and get to know each other, between training sessions.

Over the next few days, we participated in training sessions and work sessions to prepare the camp for the campers who would all arrive on Sunday. In our spare time, we took a couple excursions to Cork, Kinsale, and Ballincollig to do some sightseeing, which was enjoyable. Ireland is gorgeous, by the way. I had the opportunity to learn more about its history, which is really fascinating. Sunday, arrival day, was enjoyable, though extremely hectic.

The campers in my English program have been great and, surprisingly, very enthusiastic and participatory in the sessions we've done over the last two days. I am really enjoying them. I have students from Siberia, Russia, Italy, and France, several from Spain, and one from Tunisia. This whole camp experience has been a blast. I have had a chance to participate in the evening team-building activities and games. They have been great fun. The campers are obviously enjoying everything that is going on. The other counselors and staff here are really amazing people. I am enjoying getting to know them. They are a pretty crazy, zany, funny group of people to be around.

Before this turns into a book, I will end for now. More to come, later.

Love, Kristin

----- Original Message ----
From: CONNIE B.
Sent: Wednesday, July 16, 2008 7:14:21 p.m.
Subject: RE:)

Hi Kristin,

Sounds like you are having quite an adventure. So fun to share your dilemmas from this side of the narrative.

Connie

Wednesday, July 16, 2008 7:33 p.m.
From: "Kristin Johnson" <kristikayjohnson@yahoo.com>

Hi Connie,

It makes it fun and worthwhile to write my travel narratives when I know that people are actually reading and enjoying them. I will be writing an update in a day or so, when I have a little more time to put one together. I will keep you posted on my adventures. And thanks to all of you for praying for John and keeping an eye on him for me.

Love and miss you guys,

Kristin

I never did manage to write updates to my Europe trip. I was too busy having a blast.

Chapter Eleven

SHATTERED DREAMS OR
ONLY THE BEGINNING?

In June 2009, thousands of teaching positions were eliminated across Florida because of education budget cuts. One of them was mine. Though in my case, it was a blessing in disguise. I had been suffering from severe back pain for a dozen years or more, after being thrown from horses numerous times, and an accident in May, 1995, when I fell down an entire flight of stairs.

One of the disks at the base of my spine was obliterated. The vertebrae were left to rub against each other with a nerve pinched between them. As long as I had a job to go to, I held off from having back surgery and tried to get by with pain medication. I was miserable. In December 2009, I had back surgery and then spent the next few years recuperating.

My husband and daughters teased me endlessly because, for several months after the surgery, I became addicted to playing Farm Town and FarmVille on FaceBook. Generally, I was not motivated to do much of anything worthwhile. A "suspicious" thing happened after a few months, though. The games wouldn't load. (They still won't.) Not saying who I suspect put the kibosh on my game playing, but the message was received, loud and clear. (No, I don't think it was my husband.)

I didn't want to admit that I was dealing with major depression. My family gave me the love and support I needed to work through it. Because I wasn't able to work, and I wouldn't be able to ride horses anymore, I felt useless. I thought my dreams were dead. Of course, I was trying to pretend that I was fine, that everything was fine, but I just felt like crying all the time. I owe my poor husband, John, an eternal debt of gratitude. Because I could not bend over or carry any weight, my husband assumed most of the tasks of keeping our house clean, doing the sweeping, dusting, vacuuming, laundry, and more, while trying his best to remain positive and upbeat—even when I was being a major pain in his backside, which was often. (And I thought I was easy to live with.) I am so blessed to have such an awesome husband.

After a few months, I began feeling better and started spending more time with the Lord, talking to Him and reading His Word. He gently pulled me under the shelter of His wings, as He called me to a deeper level of repentance and commitment. He reassured me that He still had a purpose for me, and He wasn't through with me yet.

Fast forward (backtrack?) to October 2010. I don't want to spoil the ending, but okay, I will: God gave us a forty acre ranch in the Southwest on October 28, 2010. He showed it to us on October 12, 2010, and the next day, October 13th, He told us we would buy it. On December 13, 2010, our truck packed with tools and equipment, pulling a boat loaded with additional belongings, (the first load of several) and driving our Corvette, my husband and I embarked on a journey to see for the first time, the ranch that we had purchased, but never set foot on. We tendered our offer on the property four years *to the day* from when the Lord told me He would give me a ranch.

During the month of January 2011, I was staying at my mom's house, helping her recover after surgery, but was getting ready to return home to Florida. On January 27, 2011, the Lord told me to find the folder I had put His instructions in and to read them again: It was time. Then He told me to LOOK, really *look at the dates*, and think about the ranch and how we ended up with it. I clearly heard Him tell me it was time to start writing the book.

For the next several months, my husband and I divided our time between packing our household belongings and making trips back to Arizona and New Mexico. I spent several weeks trying to help pack my mother's household belongings and move them into temporary storage in preparation for moving her to the ranch in Arizona. She underwent surgery for kidney cancer in April, and her recovery was painful and slow, which made everything more difficult.

Chapter Twelve

SO HOW DO YOU WRITE A BOOK?

God told me to write a book, but I had no clue where to start. I did not even have a topic. So in March 2011, I started a journal of sorts, carrying a notebook with me everywhere I went, writing down everything that came to my mind, asking God for help and inspiration. I recorded the date, time, and sometimes the location, of every entry I wrote because He told me to do so. I include here some of the entries I wrote during that first month of beginning work on the book, fully intact. I removed them from numerous drafts because I thought readers might view them as over-the-top sappy, but for some reason, I now feel His urging to share them with you.

3/9/2011
9:45 p.m.
South Lake Hospital
Emergency Room

I started out early this morning. First thing, I had blood work done at the lab, and then my husband, John, treated me to breakfast at Cracker Barrel—all of this before 8 a.m. I've had bronchitis for the past couple weeks or so and the medicine doesn't seem to be working, so we decided I should stop by my doctor's office and see if I needed a new round of antibiotics or something else. She didn't like the sound of my lungs, so she sent me to the emergency room.

They ran ECGs, ultrasounds, and all sorts of other tests on my heart, and I am still here in the emergency room—in for the night, they say. The nurses, techs, therapists, and rest of the staff have been great, but I feel out of place and unprepared to be here. No toothbrush, comb, fresh underwear— nothing. I bled all over my shirt when they tried to put an IV in my arm. If I were at home I would be rushing around trying to get stuff done. Oh, now I get it, God. You brought me to the emergency room so I could get quiet and listen to you. I didn't bring my Bible. I did, however, bring the book I have been reading for the umpteenth time, *The God Chasers*, by Tommy Tenney. Wow. An amazing book. I highly recommend that everyone read it.

I need to repent. I need to be broken. I need to be holy because you are holy. I need to be loving because you are loving.

Dear Lord,

Please let this be a healing, cleansing night for me. Holy Spirit, please be with me now and help me to empty myself of all the things for which I need to repent. It is my heart's desire that these not be words only. I want to mean them. Please forgive me. Help me to be honest, trustworthy, loyal, and most of all, loving. Help me to love people who are unlovable, ignorant, unkempt, hateful, spiteful, mean, and vindictive. They need you just as I need you.

Please, Lord, help me to look only at myself and see the things that need to change in me. I want to worship you in spirit and in truth. I want to follow you. I want to seek your face. Help me to be a blessing to you, Lord. Thank you for everything you have done for me.

3/15/2011
4:15 p.m.

You may be wondering why I have included the date and time for many entries I write (except for when I forget!). I do this because He told me to, and because He has often given me promises that He instructed me to record, and later to note when they have been fulfilled. This "write down everything I tell you; record it and follow it" routine is new to me. I have never been in the habit of keeping a journal—a failing for which I am now deeply repentant. This could have been so much easier.

Writer's block. Lord, not even two weeks into writing this book and already, I am exhausted. I hate worrying about grammar, punctuation, capitalization, and making sure everything sounds "just right." Perhaps all this will come easier after I nap. If you tell me anything new as I nap, please help me to remember it later. Yes, there is a preposition without an object. Remind me to fix it after my nap. I am too tired to worry about it now.

Leave it alone. You are not writing an English Grammar textbook. Don't get hung up on trying to sound scholarly, lofty, or impressive. Worrying whether a participle might be dangling will only frustrate the process and slow things down. Just say what you mean, mean what you say, and write down the words I tell you to write. Simple.

I was taught to use the King's English. I don't want them thinking I don't know any better, especially my former English students (although, actually, I wish I *had* paid more attention in English class).

Grammar, punctuation, and obeying capitalization rules were never my strong suit. My approach was always, "Hey, if it looks colorful, creative, and zany, it is *okay* by me." Alas, I have a lot of unlearning to do, and no time to do it. (If you are one of my former English students, stick to what I taught you and do not do as I do.)

Focus! I AM the King. It is *my* English. Proper English is whatever *I* say it is. Trying to impress them with thees and thous, perfectly constructed sentences, and fancy words might make you feel better but it won't serve my purposes. I want people to HEAR and UNDERSTAND my message. Just make it plain, simple, and direct so even a child can understand it.

Okay, I get it. But you will have to be the one to explain it to my future editor. He's the one that will suffer migraine headaches trying to fix all my mistakes.

Just say what you mean to say. Keep it simple, plain, and direct.

Okay, got it.

3/23/2011
10:40 a.m.
Driving on I-10 to New Mexico

My husband is driving and I am enjoying the passing scenery and thinking about the devotion I just read from *The God Chasers*.

Dear Heavenly Father,

I just want you to know that I am not satisfied with where I am. You have been so good to me and blessed me abundantly with more things than I could ever have imagined, even a few short years ago. I am in awe of what you have already done in my life. I am truly grateful and thankful for what you have done for me. I want to seek your face and live in your presence. I want to sit on your lap and touch your face and tell you how much I love you. Please forgive me for the stupid, heartless, thoughtless, mean-spirited things I have done. I want my heart to be filled with love, just as your heart is filled with love. Please flood my heart with love and forgiveness for everyone in my life with whom I have ever been angry, or who hurt me. I forgive them, Father. I love them and will do what I can to let them know, and to restore them and release them in Christian love. Please help me to be the child of God, the daughter you have called me to be.

Thank you for the wonderful husband you have given me. Please help me to show him every day, how much I do love, honor, respect, and appreciate him. Help me to understand what he needs from me—the little things—and do them. Let him know that I am thinking about him. I want to please him, just as I want to please you. I value and esteem him highly. Help me to show him that he is very important to me. I need him.

Most of all, I need you. Thank you for being so good to me, forgiving me, and loving me. I trust you, believe in you, and follow you.

I love you, Lord, and I trust you. Help me to walk in your ways. I am not afraid of what the future holds because I know that you are with me. I see beautiful days ahead. I will stay by your side, sheltered in the shadow of your wings. I am chasing after you, Lord. I want to live in your presence and I am not content to live outside the Holy of Holies. I know that I cannot work my way into your presence—my deeds are worthless, filthy rags. Even so, I *am* in your presence and I rejoice in it.

Dear Lord, please fill me with your presence, your love. Please anoint me to fulfill the calling you have given to me. Please give me eyes to see and ears to hear. Please give me your wisdom, your understanding, and your knowledge. Help me to be wise as a serpent, but as harmless as a dove. Help me to walk in your truth, to worship you in spirit and truth.

Please bless my family. Please help us to come together in peace and harmony, one in spirit—your Spirit. Help us to work together to fulfill the calling you have placed on our lives. Please help us to walk in forgiveness of each other; picking each other up when we fall down, giving each other strength and support. Love covers a multitude of sins.

Please help me to forgive the people who have hurt me and to be forgiven by all the people in my life who I have hurt. Help me to restore goodwill and loving thoughts toward those people. Help me to forgive myself for the mistakes I have made in my life and be at peace with myself. Please heal me, Lord. You are Jehovah Ropheka. You are my healer. Please heal me in mind, body, and spirit. Help me to be truly yours in mind, body, and spirit.

Your eyes move to and fro, looking for those who are willing to serve you. I am willing to serve you. Help me to be sensitive to your Spirit. Help me hear your voice. I am a sheep of your pasture—I hear your voice and I know you. There is much that I do not know about you, there is a lot that I will never understand. Many things that are contained in your Word, I do not really understand because I was not there—but I do hear your voice now. You can clear things up for me as you choose to reveal them to me. You are the lamp at my feet. You will light the way and make sure that I make it safely through the valley of the shadow of death. You will make my paths straight. Lord, I accept your guidance and direction.

I accept your forgiveness, love, mercy, and your Holy Spirit as my constant companion and friend. I love you, Holy Spirit. Please forgive me for anything I have ever done to wound you or grieve you. I am truly remorseful for ever hurting, grieving, or ignoring you. I love you. Please help me to be faithful to you and please keep a tight leash on me. Don't ever let me go. I am a sheep of your pasture. I may get confused and wander off, but PLEASE don't let me go. I am yours for all eternity. Please help me to be wise and not be deceived by other voices. With ALL my heart I want to serve you and someday hear you tell me, "Well done, my good and faithful servant." You are my first love. Please help me to never forget my love for you.

I know my flesh is sinful and I know that I am unworthy. I am very afraid of meeting you. I am afraid, but yet I need you more. Please visit me, Lord, and let me experience your manifest presence. I love you.

3/24/2011
4:07 p.m.
Driving on I-10 through Texas

I just finished reading Devotion 3 from *The God Chasers* as well as the first several psalms in the Bible.

Dear Dad,

I have been thinking and reading about you all day today. It is such a beautiful day. I want you to share it with me. Katrina is driving and we are heading toward Ozona and Fort Stockton, Texas, crossing a vast expanse of desert hills, juniper trees, and QUIET. I am thinking about the idea of crawling up in your lap and turning your face toward me. I desired intimacy with you for so many years, but I didn't know how to be intimate with you, Father.

You know better than I do the reasons why it was hard for me to feel your presence. Fear, mostly—lingering remorse and sadness over so many of the mistakes I've made in my life. I know how unworthy I am and how holy you are. In my head, I know that is why Jesus died for me—because I am a sinner. And, I know I am saved by grace—but I still feel so unworthy.

I used to think that I would be happy if I could just make it to Heaven, and see you, even if from the farthest distance away—I would be content to just barely make it in. But I realize the truth is, I want more. I am not content to make it in by the skin of my teeth. I want to see your face and crawl up in your lap.

Last night, when I was talking to you, I told you how much I miss my earthly father. I lost him too soon. I miss all the father-daughter talks we used to have and I grieve for all the father-daughter talks we were never able to have. I realize that at some point, I tried to stop thinking about him anymore, because my heart used to hurt so much from the pain of missing him. The nightmares I would wake up from were terrifying, making me think he was still here somewhere, if only I could find him. It is comforting to know he is with you. It is even more comforting to know you are my Heavenly Father, and that it makes you happy when I talk to you. That is awesome. I love you, Dad, and I am so happy that I can talk to you all the time.

3/27/2011
5:33 p.m.
At the ranch,
sitting on the glider overlooking the valley,
and the Little Colorado River

Awesome Father,

Mom and I are sitting here on the glider, looking out over the vista on this beautiful ranch you have given to us. Majestic in splendor and beauty—words cannot describe how incredibly amazing your creation is. Mom and I are listening to the song, "Adonai," by Paul Wilbur. I gave Mom the book, *The God Chasers,* to read and we have been talking about it together. Funny, I am talking to you as if you haven't been here with us, listening to all of our conversations the entire time.

Talking to Mom about you and listening to her has been such a moving experience for me. Her surgery is coming up, April 6, and I know that ordinarily we would be so worried. CANCER. Scary word. But I know that you are here with us, and I know that she is going to be okay. I wish I knew how to describe all the emotions that are running through me, but I guess I don't need to. You already know. I love you Father, and I feel so much gratitude for everything you have done for me. Thank you for letting Mom and I have this special time together.

Mom and I returned to New Mexico the next week. Mom had her surgery on April 6 and spent the next few months recovering from it. I spent the next month packing boxes and more boxes, trying to empty her rental house before May 1. My husband spent the months of April and May working on the ranch, trying to turn a long neglected, rustic, far from waterproof geodesic dome, into a habitable, temporary home for my mother, my sister, and my brother. The first week in May, we both returned to Florida and spent the next several weeks finishing up packing our house.

On June 27, 2011, we began our final move from Florida to Arizona, our thirty foot moving van packed so tightly, it was nearly impossible to lift the rear cargo door. We shared the small passenger compartment with our cats, Boo and Molly, bundled in their cat carriers, and an odd assortment of anything else that wouldn't fit in the back of the moving van. We had several mishaps along the way. Even before reaching Ocala, Florida, a terrible accident ahead of us kept us at a dead standstill on I-75 for two hours. The next day, while driving through Alabama, a sheriff's deputy pulled us over for expired plates on our moving van. We had to explain that all the paperwork, including the new plates, had inadvertently been packed somewhere toward the front of the van, and there was no possibility of retrieving them until we unpacked everything in Arizona. Fortunately, he let us go.

A day or so later, while traveling through Mississippi or Arkansas somewhere, our hydraulic parking brake malfunctioned and locked up after we stopped at a Walmart parking lot, necessitating a costly service call to disable the parking brake. We were not able to have the brake repaired, so for the duration of the trip, we had to park on level ground and place blocks in front and behind each tire to keep the truck from taking a joy ride on its own.

The next day, we blew out a rear tire 100 miles before reaching Amarillo, Texas, and had to spend five hours alongside the road, waiting for help. A truck repairman brought us a used tire to replace the blown tire because that was all he had available. Three days later, 100 miles past the outskirts of Amarillo, Texas, the just-replaced used tire blew out, necessitating the costly installation of a second truck tire, this time a new one. Again, we spent five miserable hours stranded along the most barren, forlorn stretch of highway imaginable. Did I mention this was July 4th weekend and the temperatures were in the nineties, *at minimum*? Or that because we could not keep the engine running for five hours, we had no air conditioner, which meant we had to keep the windows rolled down, with two *extremely* unhappy cats closed up in their cat carriers? One of them had an accident that even copious amounts of Febreze could not help. To add to the misery, there were no bathrooms within walking distance.

A bright spot on the trip was being able to spend a couple of days visiting with friends of ours who lived in Amarillo, Texas. Otherwise, the eight day trip, which finally ended on July 6, is not a fond memory for my husband. The mere mention of it still elicits a sour look on his face and all manner of not-so-nice words from his lips.

During this stressful period of time, I was still trying to work on this book, but I was stuck and was about to give up on it. I asked God for help. He reminded me that the book was already written and then instructed me to find several papers I had written earlier, to put them together in one document in chronological order, to reread the message He had given me, and then to listen for His instructions. The book began to take shape.

Chapter Thirteen

THE JOB DESCRIPTION

"I want to help you, Lord. Tell me again, what is it you want me to do?" I said.

"Let me break it down for you. I am going to give you *your* job description, and then I will give you *my* job description."

He told me to read His message again (more carefully this time). Then He gave me the job description below.

<u>Kristin's Job Description</u>

1. Write down everything *I*, the Lord, tell you. Record it and follow it.

2. Do not hinder one another. You are the army of Joel. You will look neither to the right nor to the left but straight ahead at the task I have set before you. You will do what I have called you to do.

3. BE PREPARED.

4. Treat my people well. Pay them well.

God's Job Description

1. I will perform it.

2. I will accomplish it.

(God is like this with me—direct, plain, and simple.)

So that was it. That was (and is) my job description. Technically, should you choose to accept His call, it is your job description as well. (Is that the theme music from *Mission Impossible* I hear in my head? Listen. Can you hear it?) Yes, this mission, should you choose to accept it, will be difficult, but with His help—not impossible. In the following pages, the dream of The Shepherd's Haven will unfold.

Chapter Fourteen

THE DREAM OF THE SHEPHERD'S HAVEN

God told me to write down the vision of The Shepherd's Haven and to make it plain. What follows is the dream of The Shepherd's Haven that the Lord first showed me in August 1989. He showed me the dream, the vision as it exists in the eternal present with Him. So I share it with you in like manner.

The Shepherd's Haven

The Shepherd's Haven is a nonprofit ministry committed to sharing and imparting God's grace, love, and forgiveness to people of all ages, and to instill in their hearts the knowledge that they are special and unique. God has created them in His own likeness and image, and He loves them. He has given them special talents and abilities, and has a unique purpose for their lives. He has placed special dreams in their hearts and wants to help make them a reality. The Shepherd's Haven is also a sanctuary and haven for unwanted and abused animals.

The Mission of The Shepherd's Haven

The Shepherd's Haven will lead people to their Heavenly Father through His Son, Jesus Christ, by way of Christian education, ministry, and entertainment. The Shepherd's Haven will help every person involved discover their God-given dreams and blossom to their fullest potential.

The foundation and cornerstone of The Shepherd's Haven are made up of the values of love, grace, forgiveness, and the belief that all people are special and sacred. Every individual has a unique, God-given purpose for his or her life and talents and abilities to accomplish it (with God's help). Just as Joseph's coat was woven with many colors, God has sprinkled this planet with people of many colors and a variety of cultures, with unique perspectives to share. By culture, I mean innocuous distinctive such as clothing, food, housing, and holiday traditions—things like tacos, spaghetti, dreidles, and piñatas. Not mean, destructive, or evil acts or aspirations ("Hey Mom, I want to be a suicide bomber when I grow up").

Our loving God created all of humanity and everything that exists in this universe. Sadly, many people have a warped understanding of God and the love He has for them and all of His Creation. God's love for us has been answered with fear, distrust, abuse, and hatred which have too often led to acts of violence and murder. We insult God by blaming Him for such heinous, evil actions. We all have a lot to learn.

We must set aside our differences in religious beliefs and the resultant mistrust, hatred, and bad attitudes. God calls us to be the light of the world and show people the truth—that He loves them—and then love them as He loves us. We need to remember that God does not believe in lost causes and neither should we. That juvenile delinquent living next door to you, getting into trouble all the time and running around with a bad crowd, is probably desperately lonely, hurting, and desperate for attention. (When he is getting into trouble, at least someone is paying attention and listening to him. At least someone knows he is here, even if it's only the juvenile judge or probation officer.) He needs to know that someone—*anyone*—is interested in him, loves him, and cares about him.

Matthew 18:10-14

[10] Take heed that ye despise not one of these little ones; for I say unto you, That in heaven their angels do always behold the face of my Father which is in heaven.

[11] For the Son of man is come to save that which was lost.

[12] How think ye? if a man have an hundred sheep, and one of them be gone astray, doth he not leave the ninety and nine, and goeth into the mountains, and seeketh that which is gone astray?

[13] And if so be that he find it, verily I say unto you, he rejoiceth more of that sheep, than of the ninety and nine which went not astray.

[14] Even so it is not the will of your Father which is in heaven, that one of these little ones should perish.

It is a funny thing, the way some problems seem to linger and never go away. So many people need help, but few people are willing to help them. Just as in the time of Jesus, the harvest of people needing help is plentiful, but the laborers, indeed, are few.

Matthew 9:35-38

[35] And Jesus went about all the cities and villages, teaching in their synagogues, and preaching the gospel of the kingdom, and healing every sickness and every disease among the people.

[36] But when he saw the multitudes, he was moved with compassion on them, because they fainted, and were scattered abroad, as sheep having no shepherd.

³⁷ Then saith he unto his disciples, The harvest truly is plenteous, but the labourers are few;

³⁸ Pray ye therefore the Lord of the harvest, that he will send forth labourers into his harvest.

In the play written years ago by George Bernard Shaw, "Pygmalion," a linguistics professor, Dr. Henry Higgins, performs an experiment to see if he can help a common, uneducated flower girl, Eliza Doolittle, to transform herself into a cultured, sophisticated lady who could pass herself off as royalty. The key to the success of the experiment was that, initially, he believed in his own ability so much that he was convinced he could do it. The reality was that for the experiment to succeed, he needed Eliza Doolittle to want to change. The experiment was successful primarily because Dr. Higgins believed not only in his ability to help, but that Eliza had the ability to change. He believed in her until she could believe in herself. Another way to say it is that you will get what you expect. The greater your expectation in someone, the harder they will strive to live up to what you expect of them. Eliza so desperately wanted to better herself and improve her station in life, and receive Dr. Higgins's approval, that she was willing to work hard and sincerely commit to make great changes—a phenomenon now referred to as the Pygmalion effect.

People still talk about the Pygmalion effect. Why? Because it works. The big question is, why don't we practice what we know? Why don't we look at juvenile delinquents and emotionally troubled kids with the eyes of the heart, knowing they need someone to believe in them? They need to know they are valuable, worthwhile, and vitally important to the rest of us on this planet. They could benefit from an attitude adjustment perhaps, but they are basically made of good stuff—just as they are. They have a special contribution to make, and we need it, whether they be gifted in music, art, science, bug collecting—whatever. It may be that they need help discovering what their gifts are, but rest assured, the gifts are there. If a young person is not supported and valued, their contribution may be lost, their gift never shared. If that happens, we all lose.

Some may say that not all people are valuable, that not all can contribute something of value to society. Who among us has the omniscient perspective to make that judgment? How can we even dare to make such assumptions?

Helen Keller, Thomas Edison, Nicky Cruz (*The Cross and the Switchblade*), and dozens of others I could name all defied their own limitations or society's low opinion of their abilities, and made impressive, valuable contributions to humanity. There are many more like them in today's younger generation—even among the delinquent and emotionally troubled.

The Vision of The Shepherd's Haven

The Shepherd's Haven is actively involved in a number of activities dealing with people and animals. Any and all people who want to come to Him are welcome. The Shepherd's Haven owns ranch properties in several states and operates a number of residential treatment programs and shelters for troubled and homeless youth. As an organization, The Shepherd's Haven is on the cutting edge of innovation in alternative energy resources, agriculture, permaculture, and in using alternative building methods and materials (i.e. straw bale, cob, Earthships)—even offering training and workshops that equip people to design and build their own homes.

In addition, The Shepherd's Haven operates fully accredited educational facilities—technical and vocational (working ranch operations, etc.), and traditional—the basics of reading, writing, and arithmetic, using a *Great Books Program*, (modified for younger readers), borrowed from the program used by St. John's College in Annapolis, Maryland, and Santa Fe, New Mexico. The Shepherd's Haven sponsors a number of positive, motivational entertainment events, and a youth equestrian performing group, The Equestrianaires. The Shepherd's Haven also operates as a sanctuary and haven for unwanted and abused animals.

Chapter Fifteen

GOD'S PROVISION & BLESSING

Where does one get the money to start a ministry—especially one as involved as the one ever present in my mind and heart? For many years, I didn't know where to start. Looking at my own paltry bank account and resources was no comfort (as they were often in the red). Worry? Yes, I did worry about it. Finally, I just gave up. I gave up on the dream and mourned, thinking it would never happen and was not meant to be—it was just *too* big. Too much money, too many people, too much land—I would never be able to pull it all together. Or so I thought.

Whose Dream Is It Anyway?

Many times, I've mistakenly believed that the dream of The Shepherd's Haven came from my own mind, heart, and desires. I thought that since it was my dream, I would have to be the one to make it happen—the failure or success of getting it started rested on my shoulders. Aware of my lack of knowledge, wisdom, financial resources, and mental and physical energy, it seemed easier to just forget about it. It was a nice dream while it lasted, and it would have been great if I could have gotten it started, but it was not meant to be. I thought it was my job to make it happen. I thought it was my decision to make. Wrong!

In October 2006, God took the opportunity to set me straight.

10/13/2006
9 a.m.

I am the Boss. I am the Head. I make the decisions. Through prayer, you WILL hear my voice, I will make it *plain*. I will make this happen; I will bring it about. I will accomplish it, for it is my dream, my vision, my purpose I have given to each of you. I have called you to perform it together. Do not hinder one another. You are the army of Joel. You will look neither to the right nor to the left but straight ahead at the task I have set before you. You will do what I have called you to do.

Do not worry about money. All the money in the world is under my control. Listen to my instructions and be careful to follow them. Do not lag behind nor try to run ahead. I will go before you and come behind you—I will encompass you. I am your retirement—your exceedingly great reward. Read Deuteronomy 28. Believe it. Trust me. Am I a man that I should lie?

You are where you are right now because I led you there. You are following my plans and purposes for your life. Don't worry about hearing my voice and missing something. I can and will use anything I need to in order to make my voice heard by you—to make my wishes known to you. Don't worry about people who try to come against you. It is not a wise thing for anyone to set themselves up against my children, my anointed servants. Those who do this set themselves up against me, and I will surely deal with them according to their deeds.

Many people will serve as "lessons" in your life. You must all remember (and learn this well), that many people under your authority are serving me just as you are. Don't hinder them; empower them. Build them up. You would do well to never forget this.

Each of you, write the vision down that I have given you, make it plain. I will accomplish it. I will perform it.

10/13/2006
9:30 a.m.

Write down everything I tell you. Record it and follow it.

Be prepared. I am on the move and I will begin to send people to you, or I will send you to them. They will be ready to receive you, just as you will be ready to receive them. When they come, you will know that I have sent them.

Be prepared for the windfall. I will provide you with everything you need, *when* you need it.

Your first book will provide resources for the ranch property and I will use the book to draw the people who will come to build it. Remember Nehemiah? Is anything too hard for me?

Treat my people well. My servants—my children—are worthy of their hire. Pay them well. There will be bread in my house and NO ONE who comes to me will be hungry or thirsty.

Doctrine? Don't worry about doctrine, denominational differences, and such. If you find it in my Word (for it *is* my Word), trust it and do it. Don't waste your time arguing about it with anyone. It is simple: **Feed** my sheep. Love one another as you love yourself. If I am lifted up, I will draw all men unto *me*.

I have given the dream—the vision—to each of you. Many of you have been waiting and looking for its fulfillment for years now. As each of you begins to write down the vision you have been given, you will marvel at how similar they are. You will see the similarities and realize that it has been given to you, by me. It is from me. Your dreams and visions are my dreams and visions. They *are* one and the same. When my Word goes forth it shall NOT return to me void. It will be filled with purpose and shall accomplish everything for which I sent it.

In the beginning was the Word, and the Word was with God and the **Word** *was* God. I *was* (and am) **the Word**. I create with nothing more than **my Word**. I *need* nothing more. I spoke this world into existence. Everything that you see—and billions of things you haven't seen or even dreamed of—came into existence at MY WORD.

I speak into existence worlds and universes, yet sometimes you are afraid to trust ME. I feed and clothe the small, unseen creatures you know nothing about. I know your every thought and have numbered every hair on your head. I save your tears when you cry. Yet you have a hard time believing MY WORD—trusting that I can do BIG THINGS for you and in your life.

Yes, the vision will require a lot of money, land, and people. I know this is scary for you to think about. You have held back from starting because you feel so small, unworthy, and insignificant, doubting I would choose you and not others for this. I say, why **NOT** YOU? I have called you by name—years ago. I gave you the DREAM and you heard me (you know you heard me). Do not be like Jonah. Do NOT run away from this! Do not be like Jeremiah or Moses and give ME excuses.

I will provide everything you lack as you need it. I will be the pillar of cloud by day and the pillar of fire by night. Giants you face are not even grasshoppers to me. I laugh at them. I still sit on my throne and laugh. The nations may rage against me and come against my holy city, but they shall not prevail. My will and my Word shall NOT BE TRAMPLED UNDER. They shall stand and not be moved.

Many people will see the need to have this place for the children. As I move to bring MY PEOPLE back to me, to renew and restore their love for me, I will provide a place for ALL to come to me. I will accomplish it. For I have spoken and my Word shall go forth and accomplish my will and purpose. It only takes ONE PERSON, listening prayerfully and obediently to Me, to provide the money for the purchase of the property.

God does not make the promise that He will provide every selfish, self centered, superficial whim that we want, when we want it. He promises to provide what we truly need as we need it, to equip us to fulfill the dreams He has given to us. The emphasis is not only on material wealth and blessings, but more importantly, on spiritual blessings and true wealth—an intimate relationship with God. He promises to be our retirement, our exceedingly great reward—God, Himself is our reward, and He allows us to spend eternity with Him.

Chapter Sixteen

THE BLESSINGS OF OBEDIENCE

Speaking of Deuteronomy 28, God told me to read it, believe it, and trust Him, asking me: "Am I a man that I should lie?" So that is what I did (and do). I read it. I believe it. I trust Him. He made specific mention of it, so I take Him at His Word that Deuteronomy 28 is to be relevant today to His people, not just to the Israelites of yesteryear. It applies to me, and it applies to you. In case you are as I used to be, and spend very little time in the *Old* Testament, you'll find Deuteronomy 28 is a rather long chapter. Once again, I am asking you to pull out your Bible and read Deuteronomy 28, along with the notes and commentary that accompany it.

I include it below in the King James Version. God told me this is not a time for cut and paste, so I take this as an indication He wants it to be read in full. Verses 1 through 14 relate all the wonderful blessings God bestows upon His children when they obey Him, and are living under His covenant of grace. Then it comes to the sobering part. Verses 15 through 68 lists all the very unpleasant things that happen to people when they forsake God, are disobedient, and choose to live under the exacting demands of the law of God without God's grace and help.

Deuteronomy 28

[1]And it shall come to pass, if thou shalt hearken diligently unto the voice of the LORD thy God, to observe and to do all his commandments which I command thee this day, that the LORD thy God will set thee on high above all nations of the earth:

[2] And all these blessings shall come on thee, and overtake thee, if thou shalt hearken unto the voice of the LORD thy God.

[3] Blessed shalt thou be in the city, and blessed shalt thou be in the field.

[4] Blessed shall be the fruit of thy body, and the fruit of thy ground, and the fruit of thy cattle, the increase of thy kine, and the flocks of thy sheep.

[5] Blessed shall be thy basket and thy store.

[6] Blessed shalt thou be when thou comest in, and blessed shalt thou be when thou goest out.

[7] The LORD shall cause thine enemies that rise up against thee to be smitten before thy face: they shall come out against thee one way, and flee before thee seven ways.

[8] The LORD shall command the blessing upon thee in thy storehouses, and in all that thou settest thine hand unto; and he shall bless thee in the land which the LORD thy God giveth thee.

[9] The LORD shall establish thee an holy people unto himself, as he hath sworn unto thee, if thou shalt keep the commandments of the LORD thy God, and walk in his ways.

¹⁰ And all people of the earth shall see that thou art called by the name of the LORD; and they shall be afraid of thee.

¹¹ And the LORD shall make thee plenteous in goods, in the fruit of thy body, and in the fruit of thy cattle, and in the fruit of thy ground, in the land which the LORD sware unto thy fathers to give thee.

¹² The LORD shall open unto thee his good treasure, the heaven to give the rain unto thy land in his season, and to bless all the work of thine hand: and thou shalt lend unto many nations, and thou shalt not borrow.

¹³ And the LORD shall make thee the head, and not the tail; and thou shalt be above only, and thou shalt not be beneath; if that thou hearken unto the commandments of the LORD thy God, which I command thee this day, to observe and to do them:

¹⁴ And thou shalt not go aside from any of the words which I command thee this day, to the right hand, or to the left, to go after other gods to serve them.

¹⁵ But it shall come to pass, if thou wilt not hearken unto the voice of the LORD thy God, to observe to do all his commandments and his statutes which I command thee this day; that all these curses shall come upon thee, and overtake thee:

¹⁶ Cursed shalt thou be in the city, and cursed shalt thou be in the field.

¹⁷ Cursed shall be thy basket and thy store.

¹⁸ Cursed shall be the fruit of thy body, and the fruit of thy land, the increase of thy kine, and the flocks of thy sheep.

[19] Cursed shalt thou be when thou comest in, and cursed shalt thou be when thou goest out.

[20] The LORD shall send upon thee cursing, vexation, and rebuke, in all that thou settest thine hand unto for to do, until thou be destroyed, and until thou perish quickly; because of the wickedness of thy doings, whereby thou hast forsaken me.

[21] The LORD shall make the pestilence cleave unto thee, until he have consumed thee from off the land, whither thou goest to possess it.

[22] The LORD shall smite thee with a consumption, and with a fever, and with an inflammation, and with an extreme burning, and with the sword, and with blasting, and with mildew; and they shall pursue thee until thou perish.

[23] And thy heaven that is over thy head shall be brass, and the earth that is under thee shall be iron.

[24] The LORD shall make the rain of thy land powder and dust: from heaven shall it come down upon thee, until thou be destroyed.

[25] The LORD shall cause thee to be smitten before thine enemies: thou shalt go out one way against them, and flee seven ways before them: and shalt be removed into all the kingdoms of the earth.

[26] And thy carcase shall be meat unto all fowls of the air, and unto the beasts of the earth, and no man shall fray them away.

[27] The LORD will smite thee with the botch of Egypt, and with the emerods, and with the scab, and with the itch, whereof thou canst not be healed.

²⁸ The LORD shall smite thee with madness, and blindness, and astonishment of heart:

²⁹ And thou shalt grope at noonday, as the blind gropeth in darkness, and thou shalt not prosper in thy ways: and thou shalt be only oppressed and spoiled evermore, and no man shall save thee.

³⁰ Thou shalt betroth a wife, and another man shall lie with her: thou shalt build an house, and thou shalt not dwell therein: thou shalt plant a vineyard, and shalt not gather the grapes thereof.

³¹ Thine ox shall be slain before thine eyes, and thou shalt not eat thereof: thine ass shall be violently taken away from before thy face, and shall not be restored to thee: thy sheep shall be given unto thine enemies, and thou shalt have none to rescue them.

³² Thy sons and thy daughters shall be given unto another people, and thine eyes shall look, and fail with longing for them all the day long; and there shall be no might in thine hand.

³³ The fruit of thy land, and all thy labours, shall a nation which thou knowest not eat up; and thou shalt be only oppressed and crushed alway:

³⁴ So that thou shalt be mad for the sight of thine eyes which thou shalt see.

³⁵ The LORD shall smite thee in the knees, and in the legs, with a sore botch that cannot be healed, from the sole of thy foot unto the top of thy head.

³⁶ The LORD shall bring thee, and thy king which thou shalt set over thee, unto a nation which neither thou nor thy fathers

have known; and there shalt thou serve other gods, wood and stone.

[37] And thou shalt become an astonishment, a proverb, and a byword, among all nations whither the LORD shall lead thee.

[38] Thou shalt carry much seed out into the field, and shalt gather but little in; for the locust shall consume it.

[39] Thou shalt plant vineyards, and dress them, but shalt neither drink of the wine, nor gather the grapes; for the worms shall eat them.

[40] Thou shalt have olive trees throughout all thy coasts, but thou shalt not anoint thyself with the oil; for thine olive shall cast his fruit.

[41] Thou shalt beget sons and daughters, but thou shalt not enjoy them; for they shall go into captivity.

[42] All thy trees and fruit of thy land shall the locust consume.

[43] The stranger that is within thee shall get up above thee very high; and thou shalt come down very low.

[44] He shall lend to thee, and thou shalt not lend to him: he shall be the head, and thou shalt be the tail.

[45] Moreover all these curses shall come upon thee, and shall pursue thee, and overtake thee, till thou be destroyed; because thou hearkenedst not unto the voice of the LORD thy God, to keep his commandments and his statutes which he commanded thee:

[46] And they shall be upon thee for a sign and for a wonder, and upon thy seed for ever.

⁴⁷ Because thou servedst not the Lord thy God with joyfulness, and with gladness of heart, for the abundance of all things;

⁴⁸ Therefore shalt thou serve thine enemies which the Lord shall send against thee, in hunger, and in thirst, and in nakedness, and in want of all things: and he shall put a yoke of iron upon thy neck, until he have destroyed thee.

⁴⁹ The Lord shall bring a nation against thee from far, from the end of the earth, as swift as the eagle flieth; a nation whose tongue thou shalt not understand;

⁵⁰ A nation of fierce countenance, which shall not regard the person of the old, nor shew favour to the young:

⁵¹ And he shall eat the fruit of thy cattle, and the fruit of thy land, until thou be destroyed: which also shall not leave thee either corn, wine, or oil, or the increase of thy kine, or flocks of thy sheep, until he have destroyed thee.

⁵² And he shall besiege thee in all thy gates, until thy high and fenced walls come down, wherein thou trustedst, throughout all thy land: and he shall besiege thee in all thy gates throughout all thy land, which the Lord thy God hath given thee.

⁵³ And thou shalt eat the fruit of thine own body, the flesh of thy sons and of thy daughters, which the Lord thy God hath given thee, in the siege, and in the straitness, wherewith thine enemies shall distress thee:

⁵⁴ So that the man that is tender among you, and very delicate, his eye shall be evil toward his brother, and toward the wife of his bosom, and toward the remnant of his children which he shall leave:

⁵⁵ So that he will not give to any of them of the flesh of his children whom he shall eat: because he hath nothing left him in the siege, and in the straitness, wherewith thine enemies shall distress thee in all thy gates.

⁵⁶ The tender and delicate woman among you, which would not adventure to set the sole of her foot upon the ground for delicateness and tenderness, her eye shall be evil toward the husband of her bosom, and toward her son, and toward her daughter,

⁵⁷ And toward her young one that cometh out from between her feet, and toward her children which she shall bear: for she shall eat them for want of all things secretly in the siege and straitness, wherewith thine enemy shall distress thee in thy gates.

⁵⁸ If thou wilt not observe to do all the words of this law that are written in this book, that thou mayest fear this glorious and fearful name, THE LORD THY GOD;

⁵⁹ Then the LORD will make thy plagues wonderful, and the plagues of thy seed, even great plagues, and of long continuance, and sore sicknesses, and of long continuance.

⁶⁰ Moreover he will bring upon thee all the diseases of Egypt, which thou wast afraid of; and they shall cleave unto thee.

⁶¹ Also every sickness, and every plague, which is not written in the book of this law, them will the LORD bring upon thee, until thou be destroyed.

⁶² And ye shall be left few in number, whereas ye were as the stars of heaven for multitude; because thou wouldest not obey the voice of the LORD thy God.

⁶³ And it shall come to pass, that as the LORD rejoiced over you to do you good, and to multiply you; so the LORD will rejoice over you to destroy you, and to bring you to nought; and ye shall be plucked from off the land whither thou goest to possess it.

⁶⁴ And the LORD shall scatter thee among all people, from the one end of the earth even unto the other; and there thou shalt serve other gods, which neither thou nor thy fathers have known, even wood and stone.

⁶⁵ And among these nations shalt thou find no ease, neither shall the sole of thy foot have rest: but the LORD shall give thee there a trembling heart, and failing of eyes, and sorrow of mind:

⁶⁶ And thy life shall hang in doubt before thee; and thou shalt fear day and night, and shalt have none assurance of thy life:

⁶⁷ In the morning thou shalt say, Would God it were even! and at even thou shalt say, Would God it were morning! for the fear of thine heart wherewith thou shalt fear, and for the sight of thine eyes which thou shalt see.

⁶⁸ And the LORD shall bring thee into Egypt again with ships, by the way whereof I spake unto thee, Thou shalt see it no more again: and there ye shall be sold unto your enemies for bondmen and bondwomen, and no man shall buy you.

In case you are thinking this doesn't apply to us because this was the Old Testament, let me just remind you that in Deuteronomy

18:15-22, Moses prophesied concerning the coming of a New Prophet like Moses:

Deuteronomy 18:15-22

[15] The LORD thy God will raise up unto thee a Prophet from the midst of thee, of thy brethren, like unto me; unto him ye shall hearken;

[16] According to all that thou desiredst of the LORD thy God in Horeb in the day of the assembly, saying, Let me not hear again the voice of the LORD my God, neither let me see this great fire any more, that I die not.

[17] And the LORD said unto me, They have well spoken that which they have spoken.

[18] I will raise them up a Prophet from among their brethren, like unto thee, and will put my words in his mouth; and he shall speak unto them all that I shall command him.

[19] And it shall come to pass, that whosoever will not hearken unto my words which he shall speak in my name, I will require it of him.

[20] But the prophet, which shall presume to speak a word in my name, which I have not commanded him to speak, or that shall speak in the name of other gods, even that prophet shall die.

[21] And if thou say in thine heart, How shall we know the word which the LORD hath not spoken?

[22] When a prophet speaketh in the name of the LORD, if the thing follow not, nor come to pass, that is the thing which

the LORD hath not spoken, but the prophet hath spoken it presumptuously: thou shalt not be afraid of him. (KJV)

Jesus spoke of Deuteronomy and Moses in John 5:31-47:

John 5:31-47

[31] If I bear witness of myself, my witness is not true.

[32] There is another that beareth witness of me; and I know that the witness which he witnesseth of me is true.

[33] Ye sent unto John, and he bare witness unto the truth.

[34] But I receive not testimony from man: but these things I say, that ye might be saved.

[35] He was a burning and a shining light: and ye were willing for a season to rejoice in his light.

[36] But I have greater witness than that of John: for the works which the Father hath given me to finish, the same works that I do, bear witness of me, that the Father hath sent me.

[37] And the Father himself, which hath sent me, hath borne witness of me. Ye have neither heard his voice at any time, nor seen his shape.

[38] And ye have not his word abiding in you: for whom he hath sent, him ye believe not.

[39] Search the scriptures; for in them ye think ye have eternal life: and they are they which testify of me.

[40] And ye will not come to me, that ye might have life.

⁴¹ I receive not honour from men.

⁴² But I know you, that ye have not the love of God in you.

⁴³ I am come in my Father's name, and ye receive me not: if another shall come in his own name, him ye will receive.

⁴⁴ How can ye believe, which receive honour one of another, and seek not the honour that cometh from God only?

⁴⁵ Do not think that I will accuse you to the Father: there is one that accuseth you, even Moses, in whom ye trust.

⁴⁶ For had ye believed Moses, ye would have believed me; for he wrote of me.

⁴⁷ But if ye believe not his writings, how shall ye believe my words? (KJV)

Iesous Christos, (as pronounced in Koiné Greek), *Yeshua ha' Meshiach*, (as pronounced in Hebrew), *Jesus Christ*—take your pick— in every language, the name always points to the Anointed One, the Messiah, the Savior, the one who provides us with a second chance. In Deuteronomy 30, we are given a decision to make:

Deuteronomy 30

¹And it shall come to pass, when all these things are come upon thee, the blessing and the curse, which I have set before thee, and thou shalt call them to mind among all the nations, whither the LORD thy God hath driven thee,

² And shalt return unto the LORD thy God, and shalt obey his voice according to all that I command thee this day, thou and thy children, with all thine heart, and with all thy soul;

³ That then the LORD thy God will turn thy captivity, and have compassion upon thee, and will return and gather thee from

all the nations, whither the LORD thy God hath scattered thee.

[4] If any of thine be driven out unto the outmost parts of heaven, from thence will the LORD thy God gather thee, and from thence will he fetch thee:

[5] And the LORD thy God will bring thee into the land which thy fathers possessed, and thou shalt possess it; and he will do thee good, and multiply thee above thy fathers.

[6] And the LORD thy God will circumcise thine heart, and the heart of thy seed, to love the LORD thy God with all thine heart, and with all thy soul, that thou mayest live.

[7] And the LORD thy God will put all these curses upon thine enemies, and on them that hate thee, which persecuted thee.

[8] And thou shalt return and obey the voice of the LORD, and do all his commandments which I command thee this day.

[9] And the LORD thy God will make thee plenteous in every work of thine hand, in the fruit of thy body, and in the fruit of thy cattle, and in the fruit of thy land, for good: for the LORD will again rejoice over thee for good, as he rejoiced over thy fathers:

[10] If thou shalt hearken unto the voice of the LORD thy God, to keep his commandments and his statutes which are written in this book of the law, and if thou turn unto the LORD thy God with all thine heart, and with all thy soul.

[11] For this commandment which I command thee this day, it is not hidden from thee, neither is it far off.

[12] It is not in heaven, that thou shouldest say, Who shall go up for us to heaven, and bring it unto us, that we may hear it, and do it?

[13] Neither is it beyond the sea, that thou shouldest say, Who shall go over the sea for us, and bring it unto us, that we may hear it, and do it?

[14] But the word is very nigh unto thee, in thy mouth, and in thy heart, that thou mayest do it.

[15] See, I have set before thee this day life and good, and death and evil;

[16] In that I command thee this day to love the LORD thy God, to walk in his ways, and to keep his commandments and his statutes and his judgments, that thou mayest live and multiply: and the LORD thy God shall bless thee in the land whither thou goest to possess it.

[17] But if thine heart turn away, so that thou wilt not hear, but shalt be drawn away, and worship other gods, and serve them;

[18] I denounce unto you this day, that ye shall surely perish, and that ye shall not prolong your days upon the land, whither thou passest over Jordan to go to possess it.

[19] I call heaven and earth to record this day against you, that I have set before you life and death, blessing and cursing: therefore choose life, that both thou and thy seed may live:

[20] That thou mayest love the LORD thy God, and that thou mayest obey his voice, and that thou mayest cleave unto him: for he is thy life, and the length of thy days: that thou mayest dwell in the land which the LORD sware unto thy fathers, to Abraham, to Isaac, and to Jacob, to give them.(KJV)

The decision is yours.

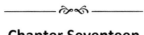

Chapter Seventeen

CONCERNING THE NATURE OF GIANTS

Sometime in early 2011, just after being reminded, but prior to my making a commitment to write this book, the LORD chided me for not trusting Him. I was letting the spirit of fear rule my life, allowing it to keep me from following Him. In so many words, He pointed out that I was so afraid of the "giants" in my life that I would rather run away from Him than fulfill the calling He had given me.

You are where you are right now because I led you there. You are following my plans and purposes for your life. Don't worry about hearing my voice and missing something. I can and will use anything I need to in order to make my voice heard by you—to make my wishes known to you. Don't worry about people who try to come against you. It is not a wise thing for anyone to set themselves up against my children, my anointed servants. Those who do this set themselves up against me, and I will surely deal with them according to their deeds.

I speak into existence worlds and universes, yet sometimes you are afraid to trust ME. I feed and clothe the small, unseen creatures you know nothing about. I know your every thought and have numbered every hair on your head. I save your tears when you cry. Yet you have a hard time believing

MY WORD—trusting that I can do BIG THINGS for you and in your life.

Yes, the vision will require a lot of money, land, and people. I know this is scary for you to think about. You have held back from starting because you feel so small, unworthy, and insignificant, doubting I would choose you and not others for this. I say, why **NOT** YOU? I have called you by name—years ago. I gave you the DREAM and you heard me (you know you heard me). Do not be like Jonah. Do NOT run away from this! Do not be like Jeremiah or Moses and give ME excuses.

I will provide everything you lack as you need it. I will be the pillar of cloud by day and the pillar of fire by night. Giants you face are not even grasshoppers to me. I laugh at them. I still sit on my throne and laugh. The nations may rage against me and come against my holy city, but they shall not prevail. My will and my Word shall NOT BE TRAMPLED UNDER. They shall stand and not be moved.

In the days of Moses, the giants were literally giants—upwards of twelve feet tall (and those were the small ones). These giants were known in Hebrew as HaNefilim, (and later, by a few other names, such as the Rephaim and Anakim, not mentioned in the foregoing passage). The word "Nefilim" or "Nephilim" is the noun form that comes from a Hebrew root word meaning "to fall," and means, "the fallen ones," or "the ones who fell."

First mentioned in Bereshis 6/Genesis 6, verse 4, the HaNefilim, the offspring of the bnei HaElohim (sons of God) and the banot HaAdam (daughters of Adam/men), are spoken of as *Gibborim,* "which were of old, men of renown." Some people interpret the phrase "sons of God" as referring to the line of Seth, being godly. They interpret "daughters of men," as referring to Cain's descendants, being ungodly and therefore of men. However, this interpretation would not explain the increased stature and abilities of the giants, or the curious appellation *HaNefilim—the fallen ones.* Where did they fall from and why?

The Hebrew language makes it very clear that fallen sons of God, or angels, disobeyed God and left their "first estate," and bore children with human women—children that were genetic angel/human hybrids. With their increased stature, appetites, and capabilities that surpassed those of genetically pure human beings, they earned the reputation of "men of renown." "Men of renown" sounds positive and good, and normally the word does have a positive connotation, but in this case, the Gibborim being spoken of were quite the opposite.

Bereshis 6

¹And it came to pass, when HaAdam began to multiply on the face of ha'adamah, and banot were born unto them,

² That the bnei HaElohim saw the banot HaAdam that they were tovot; and they took them nashim of all which they chose.

³ And Hashem said, My Ruach [Hakodesh] shall not always strive with Adam, for that he also is basar: yet his yamim shall be a hundred and twenty shanah.

⁴ HaNefilim were on ha'aretz in those yamim; and also after that, when the bnei HaElohim came in unto the banot HaAdam, and they bore children to them, the same became gibborim which were of old, men of renown.

⁵ And Hashem saw that the wickedness of HaAdam was great in ha'aretz and that every yetzer (inclination) of the machshevot (thoughts) of his lev was only rah (evil) continually.

⁶ And Hashem relented that He had made HaAdam on ha'aretz, and He was hurt in His lev.

⁷ And Hashem said, I will wipe out HaAdam whom I have created from the face of ha'adamah; both Adam, and Behemah, and the Remes and the Oph HaShomayim; for I relent that I have made them.

⁸ But Noach found chen (grace, unmerited favor) in the eyes of Hashem. (OJB)

Rephrased in the more familiar King James Version, (which translates the Hebrew words into English), the same text reads:

Genesis 6

¹And it came to pass, when men began to multiply on the face of the earth, and daughters were born unto them,

² That the sons of God saw the daughters of men that they were fair; and they took them wives of all which they chose.

³ And the LORD said, My spirit shall not always strive with man, for that he also is flesh: yet his days shall be an hundred and twenty years.

⁴ There were giants in the earth in those days; and also after that, when the sons of God came in unto the daughters of men, and they bare children to them, the same became mighty men which were of old, men of renown.

⁵ And God saw that the wickedness of man was great in the earth, and that every imagination of the thoughts of his heart was only evil continually.

⁶ And it repented the LORD that he had made man on the earth, and it grieved him at his heart.

⁷ And the LORD said, I will destroy man whom I have created from the face of the earth; both man, and beast, and the creeping thing, and the fowls of the air; for it repenteth me that I have made them.

⁸ But Noah found grace in the eyes of the LORD.

In Jude 1:6, Jude alludes to the angels who left their own habitation and disobeyed God by not keeping their first estate and taking the daughters of men as their wives:

Jude 1:6

⁶ And the angels which kept not their first estate, but left their own habitation, he hath reserved in everlasting chains under darkness unto the judgment of the great day.

These giants (HaNefilim) were *very* bad people, descendants of Canaan who had been cursed by his grandfather, Noah. (We'll save that story for another day.)

I want to give you a little more detail about one of them—Og, king of Bashan—by sharing an account of him found in Deuteronomy 3 and later, again in Deuteronomy 31. Just to give you a heads up, the scripture notes that only Og, king of Bashan, remained of the remnant of the giants, (in Hebrew, Rephaim), and that his bedstead was an iron bedstead nine cubits in length and four cubits in width, according to the standard cubit, which is approximately 18 inches. In other words, Og, king of Bashan, required a bed almost fourteen feet long! (Yes, you read that correctly, *fourteen feet!* It's amazing what you can discover in the Bible, isn't it?)

Deuteronomy 3:1-22

¹Then we turned, and went up the way to Bashan: and Og the king of Bashan came out against us, he and all his people, to battle at Edrei.

² And the LORD said unto me, Fear him not: for I will deliver him, and all his people, and his land, into thy hand; and thou shalt do unto him as thou didst unto Sihon king of the Amorites, which dwelt at Heshbon.

³ So the LORD our God delivered into our hands Og also, the king of Bashan, and all his people: and we smote him until none was left to him remaining.

⁴ And we took all his cities at that time, there was not a city which we took not from them, threescore cities, all the region of Argob, the kingdom of Og in Bashan.

⁵ All these cities were fenced with high walls, gates, and bars; beside unwalled towns a great many.

⁶ And we utterly destroyed them, as we did unto Sihon king of Heshbon, utterly destroying the men, women, and children, of every city.

⁷ But all the cattle, and the spoil of the cities, we took for a prey to ourselves.

⁸ And we took at that time out of the hand of the two kings of the Amorites the land that was on this side Jordan, from the river of Arnon unto mount Hermon;

⁹ (Which Hermon the Sidonians call Sirion; and the Amorites call it Shenir;)

¹⁰ All the cities of the plain, and all Gilead, and all Bashan, unto Salchah and Edrei, cities of the kingdom of Og in Bashan.

¹¹ For only Og king of Bashan remained of the remnant of giants; behold his bedstead was a bedstead of iron; is it not in Rabbath of the children of Ammon? nine cubits was the length thereof, and four cubits the breadth of it, after the cubit of a man.

¹² And this land, which we possessed at that time, from Aroer, which is by the river Arnon, and half mount Gilead, and the cities thereof, gave I unto the Reubenites and to the Gadites.

¹³ And the rest of Gilead, and all Bashan, being the kingdom of Og, gave I unto the half tribe of Manasseh; all the region of Argob, with all Bashan, which was called the land of giants.

¹⁴ Jair the son of Manasseh took all the country of Argob unto the coasts of Geshuri and Maachathi; and called them after his own name, Bashanhavothjair, unto this day.

¹⁵ And I gave Gilead unto Machir.

¹⁶ And unto the Reubenites and unto the Gadites I gave from Gilead even unto the river Arnon half the valley, and the border even unto the river Jabbok, which is the border of the children of Ammon;

¹⁷ The plain also, and Jordan, and the coast thereof, from Chinnereth even unto the sea of the plain, even the salt sea, under Ashdothpisgah eastward.

¹⁸ And I commanded you at that time, saying, The LORD your God hath given you this land to possess it: ye shall pass over armed before your brethren the children of Israel, all that are meet for the war.

[19] But your wives, and your little ones, and your cattle, (for I know that ye have much cattle,) shall abide in your cities which I have given you;

[20] Until the LORD have given rest unto your brethren, as well as unto you, and until they also possess the land which the LORD your God hath given them beyond Jordan: and then shall ye return every man unto his possession, which I have given you.

[21] And I commanded Joshua at that time, saying, Thine eyes have seen all that the LORD your God hath done unto these two kings: so shall the LORD do unto all the kingdoms whither thou passest.

[22] Ye shall not fear them: for the LORD your God he shall fight for you. (KJV)

Moses again speaks of Og, king of Bashan, in Deuteronomy 31 wherein he reminded the Israelites to be strong and of good courage, and to not be afraid of the people in the nations they were going in to dispossess, because God would be with them, and would not leave or forsake them.

Deuteronomy 31:1-8

[1] And Moses went and spake these words unto all Israel.

[2] And he said unto them, I am an hundred and twenty years old this day; I can no more go out and come in: also the LORD hath said unto me, Thou shalt not go over this Jordan.

[3] The LORD thy God, he will go over before thee, and he will destroy these nations from before thee, and thou shalt possess them: and Joshua, he shall go over before thee, as the LORD hath said.

⁴ And the LORD shall do unto them as he did to Sihon and to Og, kings of the Amorites, and unto the land of them, whom he destroyed.

⁵ And the LORD shall give them up before your face, that ye may do unto them according unto all the commandments which I have commanded you.

⁶ Be strong and of a good courage, fear not, nor be afraid of them: for the LORD thy God, he it is that doth go with thee; he will not fail thee, nor forsake thee.

⁷ And Moses called unto Joshua, and said unto him in the sight of all Israel, Be strong and of a good courage: for thou must go with this people unto the land which the LORD hath sworn unto their fathers to give them; and thou shalt cause them to inherit it.

⁸ And the LORD, he it is that doth go before thee; he will be with thee, he will not fail thee, neither forsake thee: fear not, neither be dismayed. (KJV)

Whatever or *whoever* your giants are, the LORD Himself promises to cross over before you and destroy them. To Him, they are just grasshoppers, after all—*little, itty-bitty grasshoppers.*

Okay, I feel better now.

Chapter Eighteen

THE ARMY OF JOEL

As I have already confessed, until a few years ago, I had not spent much time reading or studying the Old Testament, especially books such as Leviticus and Deuteronomy. I read through most, if not all, the Old Testament, when I was in college, before I became a Christian, but I did not understand it—any of it. Even after I became a Christian, a long period of time passed before I tried to read through the Old Testament again. On those occasions when I felt so inspired, I would start at Genesis and read through Exodus, doing pretty well. But by the time I read through Leviticus and Deuteronomy, I was ready to give up. I couldn't keep track of who was who, and how many horses, donkeys, goats, and wives they had, or why I should care.

I mistakenly thought that it was no longer relevant. The Old Testament, I thought, was the "Old Covenant" of burnt offerings and sacrifices before the Messiah (Christ) had come, and now that He had, we were under the "New Covenant" of grace. I figured all the burnt offerings, sacrifices, ancient customs, and laws no longer applied to us. I didn't think the Old Testament was important, and because I didn't understand it, I took the lazy way out and just didn't read it, thinking it was boring. (Though I had never verbally made a statement to that effect, not even to myself, it was just another one of those unspoken thoughts in my head.)

I had not yet developed the knack for asking God to explain what everything meant and why it was important. God told me that reading the Old Testament is important because we need to know what the law of God is, and why living under God's grace is preferable. We need to be reminded that there is only one important decision in life we need to make and that we have only two choices. Do you want to live your life bound by the law and its consequences, (i.e. burnt offerings, sacrifices, and the law of Moses), or do you want to live under God's grace? I bring this up only because the Lord reminded me of a conversation we had regarding whether or not I should include in this book a very long academic paper I had written as a graduate student at Drake University, entitled, "The Wacky World of Implementation."

In the paper, I explored the juvenile justice system and ways of implementing juvenile justice policies that might improve the lives of young people. It was over one hundred pages long, so it is difficult to give you a one sentence synopsis of the paper. The discussion I had with the Lord was whether I should include the paper or not, because I felt it was very boring, pedantic, and technical. This was His response:

> Some people think that Deuteronomy and Leviticus are boring, but you will notice that they are still in MY WORD. The importance and worth of something is not determined or dictated by whether or not it is perceived by others to be "boring." That paper contains much of the vision I gave to you all those years ago, including much of the history of that time in your life and the experiences you had as you began to learn about Me and get to know Me. It is a record of our relationship. It is for you to remember, and it is for others to know that I **AM** always **HERE** and **NOW**. For those who have eyes, let them see; those who have ears, let them hear.

(Ouch. Once again, He knew exactly what I had been thinking.) The paper stayed in the draft manuscript all the way through the first round of editing. But then, realizing I did not have the ability to go back and find all of the resource materials to check and double-check that everything was accurate, and to be able to seek permission to include them in this book, the Lord and I decided to compromise. I removed the paper, but incorporated some of the best parts throughout the book.

Before God gave me the message in October, 2006, the Book of Joel was one of the books in the Old Testament to which I had not paid much attention, so I did not know, or remember, why God would reference the army of Joel. So I read it.

The Book of Joel describes a time when the land had been laid waste, and there was mourning for the land of the people of Judah. The Lord was destroying them because of their transgressions against Him. The Day of the Lord was coming. The Lord called His people to repentance. (For those who do not have access to a Bible, I include it here in full):

Joel 1

¹The word of the LORD that came to Joel the son of Pethuel.

² Hear this, ye old men, and give ear, all ye inhabitants of the land. Hath this been in your days, or even in the days of your fathers?

³ Tell ye your children of it, and let your children tell their children, and their children another generation.

⁴ That which the palmerworm hath left hath the locust eaten; and that which the locust hath left hath the cankerworm eaten; and that which the cankerworm hath left hath the caterpiller eaten.

⁵ Awake, ye drunkards, and weep; and howl, all ye drinkers of wine, because of the new wine; for it is cut off from your mouth.

⁶ For a nation is come up upon my land, strong, and without number, whose teeth are the teeth of a lion, and he hath the cheek teeth of a great lion.

⁷ He hath laid my vine waste, and barked my fig tree: he hath made it clean bare, and cast it away; the branches thereof are made white.

⁸ Lament like a virgin girded with sackcloth for the husband of her youth.

⁹ The meat offering and the drink offering is cut off from the house of the LORD; the priests, the LORD's ministers, mourn.

¹⁰ The field is wasted, the land mourneth; for the corn is wasted: the new wine is dried up, the oil languisheth.

¹¹ Be ye ashamed, O ye husbandmen; howl, O ye vinedressers, for the wheat and for the barley; because the harvest of the field is perished.

¹² The vine is dried up, and the fig tree languisheth; the pomegranate tree, the palm tree also, and the apple tree, even all the trees of the field, are withered: because joy is withered away from the sons of men.

¹³ Gird yourselves, and lament, ye priests: howl, ye ministers of the altar: come, lie all night in sackcloth, ye ministers of my God: for the meat offering and the drink offering is withholden from the house of your God.

¹⁴ Sanctify ye a fast, call a solemn assembly, gather the elders and all the inhabitants of the land into the house of the LORD your God, and cry unto the LORD,

¹⁵ Alas for the day! for the day of the LORD is at hand, and as a destruction from the Almighty shall it come.

¹⁶ Is not the meat cut off before our eyes, yea, joy and gladness from the house of our God?

¹⁷ The seed is rotten under their clods, the garners are laid desolate, the barns are broken down; for the corn is withered.

¹⁸ How do the beasts groan! the herds of cattle are perplexed, because they have no pasture; yea, the flocks of sheep are made desolate.

¹⁹ O LORD, to thee will I cry: for the fire hath devoured the pastures of the wilderness, and the flame hath burned all the trees of the field.

²⁰ The beasts of the field cry also unto thee: for the rivers of waters are dried up, and the fire hath devoured the pastures of the wilderness.

Joel 2

¹Blow ye the trumpet in Zion, and sound an alarm in my holy mountain: let all the inhabitants of the land tremble: for the day of the LORD cometh, for it is nigh at hand;

² A day of darkness and of gloominess, a day of clouds and of thick darkness, as the morning spread upon the mountains: a great people and a strong; there hath not been ever the like, neither shall be any more after it, even to the years of many generations.

³ A fire devoureth before them; and behind them a flame burneth: the land is as the garden of Eden before them, and behind them a desolate wilderness; yea, and nothing shall escape them.

⁴ The appearance of them is as the appearance of horses; and as horsemen, so shall they run.

⁵ Like the noise of chariots on the tops of mountains shall they leap, like the noise of a flame of fire that devoureth the stubble, as a strong people set in battle array.

⁶ Before their face the people shall be much pained: all faces shall gather blackness.

⁷ They shall run like mighty men; they shall climb the wall like men of war; and they shall march every one on his ways, and they shall not break their ranks:

⁸ Neither shall one thrust another; they shall walk every one in his path: and when they fall upon the sword, they shall not be wounded.

⁹ They shall run to and fro in the city; they shall run upon the wall, they shall climb up upon the houses; they shall enter in at the windows like a thief.

¹⁰ The earth shall quake before them; the heavens shall tremble: the sun and the moon shall be dark, and the stars shall withdraw their shining:

¹¹ And the LORD shall utter his voice before his army: for his camp is very great: for he is strong that executeth his word: for the day of the LORD is great and very terrible; and who can abide it?

¹² Therefore also now, saith the LORD, turn ye even to me with all your heart, and with fasting, and with weeping, and with mourning:

¹³ And rend your heart, and not your garments, and turn unto the LORD your God: for he is gracious and merciful, slow to anger, and of great kindness, and repenteth him of the evil.

[14] Who knoweth if he will return and repent, and leave a blessing behind him; even a meat offering and a drink offering unto the LORD your God?

[15] Blow the trumpet in Zion, sanctify a fast, call a solemn assembly:

[16] Gather the people, sanctify the congregation, assemble the elders, gather the children, and those that suck the breasts: let the bridegroom go forth of his chamber, and the bride out of her closet.

[17] Let the priests, the ministers of the LORD, weep between the porch and the altar, and let them say, Spare thy people, O LORD, and give not thine heritage to reproach, that the heathen should rule over them: wherefore should they say among the people, Where is their God?

[18] Then will the LORD be jealous for his land, and pity his people.

[19] Yea, the LORD will answer and say unto his people, Behold, I will send you corn, and wine, and oil, and ye shall be satisfied therewith: and I will no more make you a reproach among the heathen:

[20] But I will remove far off from you the northern army, and will drive him into a land barren and desolate, with his face toward the east sea, and his hinder part toward the utmost sea, and his stink shall come up, and his ill savour shall come up, because he hath done great things.

[21] Fear not, O land; be glad and rejoice: for the LORD will do great things.

²² Be not afraid, ye beasts of the field: for the pastures of the wilderness do spring, for the tree beareth her fruit, the fig tree and the vine do yield their strength.

²³ Be glad then, ye children of Zion, and rejoice in the LORD your God: for he hath given you the former rain moderately, and he will cause to come down for you the rain, the former rain, and the latter rain in the first month.

²⁴ And the floors shall be full of wheat, and the vats shall overflow with wine and oil.

²⁵ And I will restore to you the years that the locust hath eaten, the cankerworm, and the caterpiller, and the palmerworm, my great army which I sent among you.

²⁶ And ye shall eat in plenty, and be satisfied, and praise the name of the LORD your God, that hath dealt wondrously with you: and my people shall never be ashamed.

²⁷ And ye shall know that I am in the midst of Israel, and that I am the LORD your God, and none else: and my people shall never be ashamed.

²⁸ And it shall come to pass afterward, that I will pour out my spirit upon all flesh; and your sons and your daughters shall prophesy, your old men shall dream dreams, your young men shall see visions:

²⁹ And also upon the servants and upon the handmaids in those days will I pour out my spirit.

³⁰ And I will shew wonders in the heavens and in the earth, blood, and fire, and pillars of smoke.

[31] The sun shall be turned into darkness, and the moon into blood, before the great and terrible day of the LORD come.

[32] And it shall come to pass, that whosoever shall call on the name of the LORD shall be delivered: for in mount Zion and in Jerusalem shall be deliverance, as the LORD hath said, and in the remnant whom the LORD shall call.

Joel 3

[1] For, behold, in those days, and in that time, when I shall bring again the captivity of Judah and Jerusalem,

[2] I will also gather all nations, and will bring them down into the valley of Jehoshaphat, and will plead with them there for my people and for my heritage Israel, whom they have scattered among the nations, and parted my land.

[3] And they have cast lots for my people; and have given a boy for an harlot, and sold a girl for wine, that they might drink.

[4] Yea, and what have ye to do with me, O Tyre, and Zidon, and all the coasts of Palestine? will ye render me a recompence? and if ye recompense me, swiftly and speedily will I return your recompence upon your own head;

[5] Because ye have taken my silver and my gold, and have carried into your temples my goodly pleasant things:

[6] The children also of Judah and the children of Jerusalem have ye sold unto the Grecians, that ye might remove them far from their border.

⁷ Behold, I will raise them out of the place whither ye have sold them, and will return your recompence upon your own head:

⁸ And I will sell your sons and your daughters into the hand of the children of Judah, and they shall sell them to the Sabeans, to a people far off: for the LORD hath spoken it.

⁹ Proclaim ye this among the Gentiles; Prepare war, wake up the mighty men, let all the men of war draw near; let them come up:

¹⁰ Beat your plowshares into swords and your pruninghooks into spears: let the weak say, I am strong.

¹¹ Assemble yourselves, and come, all ye heathen, and gather yourselves together round about: thither cause thy mighty ones to come down, O LORD.

¹² Let the heathen be wakened, and come up to the valley of Jehoshaphat: for there will I sit to judge all the heathen round about.

¹³ Put ye in the sickle, for the harvest is ripe: come, get you down; for the press is full, the fats overflow; for their wickedness is great.

¹⁴ Multitudes, multitudes in the valley of decision: for the day of the LORD is near in the valley of decision.

¹⁵ The sun and the moon shall be darkened, and the stars shall withdraw their shining.

¹⁶ The LORD also shall roar out of Zion, and utter his voice from Jerusalem; and the heavens and the earth shall shake: but the

LORD will be the hope of his people, and the strength of the children of Israel.

¹⁷ So shall ye know that I am the LORD your God dwelling in Zion, my holy mountain: then shall Jerusalem be holy, and there shall no strangers pass through her any more.

¹⁸ And it shall come to pass in that day, that the mountains shall drop down new wine, and the hills shall flow with milk, and all the rivers of Judah shall flow with waters, and a fountain shall come forth out of the house of the LORD, and shall water the valley of Shittim.

¹⁹ Egypt shall be a desolation, and Edom shall be a desolate wilderness, for the violence against the children of Judah, because they have shed innocent blood in their land.

²⁰ But Judah shall dwell for ever, and Jerusalem from generation to generation.

²¹ For I will cleanse their blood that I have not cleansed: for the LORD dwelleth in Zion. (KJV)

Once again, I encourage you to pull out your Bible and read the commentary and notes which offer additional insight. You may already know this, but in Hebrew, the name, Joel, means "Yahweh is God." As for what God means by telling us we are the army of Joel, or why He feels it is important to draw our attention to the Book of Joel, I will leave you to draw your own conclusions.

Chapter Nineteen

THE DREAM COMES CLOSER TO REALITY

My husband, John, my mother, Claudia, my sister, Julyne, and I have been living on The Shepherd's Haven Ranch since July 2011, and have been working to develop it since that time, trying to return a hodgepodge of ramshackle, old buildings into waterproof, useful structures—barns, chicken coop, rabbit hutch, greenhouse, a geodesic dome, and all. We are also trying to build a home to live in so we can escape the confines of the much too tiny thirty foot trailer we have been sharing with Boo and Molly (our spoiled rotten felines), and a jillion of my books that I simply cannot give up, since we moved here in July 2011.

There are wonderful, amazing ministries and churches in every town, city, and locale all over the earth, as our Shepherd has many havens. There are even numerous ministries with Shepherd's Haven in their name, or some variant of it. I encourage you to support them. Even so, there are still countless people out there who need help, and more people are needed to help them. God has chosen people to be a part of this ministry to help them. He knows who you are.

Many of us are cautious and leery about contributing resources—financial and otherwise—because there has been a lot of abuse, even in well-known ministries. I would just like to say that the quality time you invest in the life of one person (or more), who do not yet know the love of God, and need your help, cannot be abused or wasted. The love of God that you share with them will not return void and the results are eternal. When you give of yourself, your time, and talent, you will see the results. If you give financially and/or materially, involve yourself to ensure that your gift is used responsibly. We are all responsible for the honesty and integrity of our lives and any ministry we undertake in the name of God. We are all accountable to each other to be blameless, faithful stewards of the resources God has entrusted to us.

Reason tells us that aerodynamically, the bumblebee should not be able to fly. His body is too large and his wings are too small. But the bumblebee doesn't worry about reason or logic. The good Lord made him the way he is, intending for him to fly, and so he does.

When you do God's will, in God's way, you have at your disposal His resources—with God, *all* things are possible. With God's help, this can work, so let us continue to dream, plan, strive, and build. Allow God to make His dreams for you come true. Just as in the times of Nehemiah, when the Lord called His people to build a wall around His holy city, He is calling us to build The Shepherd's Haven, where God's lost sheep can come to seek His face and learn to love and minister to one another, practicing the words found in 1 Corinthians 13:

1 Corinthians 13

[1]Though I speak with the tongues of men and of angels, and have not charity, I am become as sounding brass, or a tinkling cymbal.

[2] And though I have the gift of prophecy, and understand all mysteries, and all knowledge; and though I have all faith, so

that I could remove mountains, and have not charity, I am nothing.

³ And though I bestow all my goods to feed the poor, and though I give my body to be burned, and have not charity, it profiteth me nothing.

⁴ Charity suffereth long, and is kind; charity envieth not; charity vaunteth not itself, is not puffed up,

⁵ Doth not behave itself unseemly, seeketh not her own, is not easily provoked, thinketh no evil;

⁶ Rejoiceth not in iniquity, but rejoiceth in the truth;

⁷ Beareth all things, believeth all things, hopeth all things, endureth all things.

⁸ Charity never faileth: but whether there be prophecies, they shall fail; whether there be tongues, they shall cease; whether there be knowledge, it shall vanish away.

⁹ For we know in part, and we prophesy in part.

¹⁰ But when that which is perfect is come, then that which is in part shall be done away.

¹¹ When I was a child, I spake as a child, I understood as a child, I thought as a child: but when I became a man, I put away childish things.

¹² For now we see through a glass, darkly; but then face to face: now I know in part; but then shall I know even as also I am known.

[13] And now abideth faith, hope, charity, these three; but the greatest of these is charity. (KJV)

The Lord will accomplish His will and purpose for The Shepherd's Haven. One final time, I leave you with His words...

10/13/2006
9 a.m.

I am the Boss. I am the Head. I make the decisions. Through prayer, you WILL hear my voice, I will make it *plain*. I will make this happen; I will bring it about. I will accomplish it, for it is my dream, my vision, my purpose I have given to each of you. I have called you to perform it together. Do not hinder one another. You are the army of Joel. You will look neither to the right nor to the left but straight ahead at the task I have set before you. You will do what I have called you to do.

Do not worry about money. All the money in the world is under my control. Listen to my instructions and be careful to follow them. Do not lag behind nor try to run ahead. I will go before you and come behind you—I will encompass you. I am your retirement—your exceedingly great reward. Read Deuteronomy 28. Believe it. Trust me. Am I a man that I should lie?

You are where you are right now because I led you there. You are following my plans and purposes for your life. Don't worry about hearing my voice and missing something. I can and will use anything I need to in order to make my voice heard by you—to make my wishes known to you. Don't worry about people who try to come against you. It is not a wise thing for anyone to set themselves up against my children, my anointed servants. Those who do this set themselves up against me, and I will surely deal with them according to their deeds.

Many people will serve as "lessons" in your life. You must all remember (and learn this well), that many people under your authority are serving me just as you are. Don't hinder them; empower them. Build them up. You would do well to never forget this.

Each of you, write the vision down that I have given you, make it plain. I will accomplish it. I will perform it.

10/13/2006
9:30 a.m.

Write down everything I tell you. Record it and follow it.

Be prepared. I am on the move and I will begin to send people to you, or I will send you to them. They will be ready to receive you, just as you will be ready to receive them. When they come, you will know that I have sent them.

Be prepared for the windfall. I will provide you with everything you need, *when* you need it.

Your first book will provide resources for the ranch property and I will use the book to draw the people who will come to build it. Remember Nehemiah? Is anything too hard for me?

Treat my people well. My servants—my children—are worthy of their hire. Pay them well. There will be bread in my house and NO ONE who comes to me will be hungry or thirsty.

Doctrine? Don't worry about doctrine, denominational differences, and such. If you find it in my Word (for it *is* my Word), trust it and do it. Don't waste your time arguing about it with anyone. It is simple: **Feed** my sheep. Love one another as you love yourself. If I am lifted up, I will draw all men unto *me*.

I have given the dream—the vision—to each of you. Many of you have been waiting and looking for its fulfillment for years now. As each of you begins to write down the vision you have been given, you will marvel at how similar they are. You will see the similarities and realize that it has been given to you, by me. It is from me. Your dreams and visions are my dreams and visions. They *are* one and the same. When my Word goes forth it shall NOT return to me void. It will be filled with purpose and shall accomplish everything for which I sent it.

In the beginning was the Word, and the Word was with God and the **Word** *was* God. I *was* (and am) **the Word**. I create with nothing more than **my Word**. I *need* nothing more. I spoke this world into existence. Everything that you see—and billions of things you haven't seen or even dreamed of—came into existence at MY WORD.

I speak into existence worlds and universes, yet sometimes you are afraid to trust ME. I feed and clothe the small, unseen creatures you know nothing about. I know your every thought and have numbered every hair on your head. I save your tears when you cry. Yet you have a hard time believing MY WORD—trusting that I can do BIG THINGS for you and in your life.

Yes, the vision will require a lot of money, land, and people. I know this is scary for you to think about. You have held back from starting because you feel so small, unworthy, and insignificant, doubting I would choose you and not others for this. I say, why *NOT* YOU? I have called you by name—years ago. I gave you the DREAM and you heard me (you know you heard me). Do not be like Jonah. Do NOT run away from this! Do not be like Jeremiah or Moses and give ME excuses.

I will provide everything you lack as you need it. I will be the pillar of cloud by day and the pillar of fire by night. Giants you face are not even grasshoppers to me. I laugh at them. I still sit on my throne and laugh. The nations may rage against me and come against my holy city, but they shall not prevail. My will and my Word shall NOT BE TRAMPLED UNDER. They shall stand and not be moved.

10/13/2006
2:05 p.m.

Remember what I spoke to you all those years ago. Write it again and hold to it. Remember it!

Many people will see the need to have this place for the children. As I move to bring MY PEOPLE back to me, to renew and restore their love for me, I will provide a place for ALL to come to me. I will accomplish it. For I have spoken and my Word shall go forth and accomplish my will and purpose. It only takes ONE PERSON, listening prayerfully and obediently to Me, to provide the money for the purchase of the property.

Those of you I have spoken to—and you know who you are—commit and set aside time to pray together diligently and earnestly for the vision to come to pass. As I provide guidance and direction, OPENING DOORS, AVENUES, and HIGHWAYS, be SURE to step out in faith and follow me. Do you have faith even as small as a mustard seed? If so, watch it grow and bloom and flourish—even as the cedars of Lebanon.

Trust me. Watch and walk in faith. You are a story in the Bible. You are writing it NOW. What will it say? Will it say that you believed me? Yes! You will walk in faith. Believe in me—my Word is truth.

The first book He told me I would write has now been published and released on October 13, 2013, seven years to the day from when the Lord first gave me His message. You now hold it in your hands, digitally or on paper. As He frequently reminds me:

I am the Boss. I am the Head. I make the decisions. Through prayer, you WILL hear my voice, I will make it *plain*. I will make this happen; I will bring it about. I will accomplish it, for it is my dream, my vision, my purpose I have given to each of you. I have called you to perform it together. Do not hinder one another. You are the army of Joel. You will look neither to the right nor to the left but straight ahead at the task I have set before you. You will do what I have called you to do.

Yes, God is the Boss. He is the Head, and He makes all of the decisions. I do not know exactly what He plans to bring about and accomplish, or when He plans to do it, but I know that everything will happen according to His will, in His time. These words I penned seven years ago were *His words*, not mine. My giants are only grasshoppers in His path, and the battle is His. I could make it longer and more complicated, but to what purpose?

The Shepherd's Haven has yet to be built, and the rest of this story has yet to be written. Will you be a chapter in its pages? I ask you, has the Lord been speaking to you? Do you "know who you are"? Have you been waiting for years for your vision to come to pass? If you can see yourself in these pages, then these words were written for you. Listen for His instructions and follow them. You will know what to do. I leave you with my email address and will be waiting to hear from you at theshepherdshavenbook@gmail.com, or you can call or write to me at:

Kristin Johnson
The Shepherd's Haven
H.C. 65, Box 34201
Concho, AZ 85924
928-821-6335
FaceBook: Kristin Johnson
Twitter: @kkstargazer1
YouTube: www.youtube.com/user/ShepherdsHavenBook
www.theshepherdshaven.com

CPSIA information can be obtained at www.ICGtesting.com
Printed in the USA
LVOW13s0228010514

383989LV00003B/97/P